My Neighbor Jesus

In the Light of His Own Language, People, and Time

by
GEORGE M. LAMSA

With a Prefatory Note by
HENRY WYSHAM LANIER

HARPER & BROTHERS PUBLISHERS
New York and London

*This book
is affectionately dedicated
to*
John A. Roebling
*with deepest appreciation
for his interest
in preserving the language
of our Lord*

Contents

	Prefatory Note	ix
	Introduction	xiii
I.	Nearer to Jesus	1
II.	God Our Father	11
III.	The Healer	18
IV.	A Test Case	32
V.	The Courageous Challenge	37
VI.	True Treasure	48
VII.	Oriental Hospitality	55
VIII.	Rich Men	59
IX.	"Let the Dead Bury the Dead"	68
X.	Days of Gloom	73

XI.	At the Gate	85
XII.	Washing the Feet	97
XIII.	The Betrayal	104
XIV.	Before Pilate	122
XV.	On the Cross	129
XVI.	The Resurrection	140

Prefatory Note

The author of this book is an Assyrian.

His people, now struggling for bare existence in a non-fertile corner of Iraq, are the pitiful surviving remnant of that conquering race which for thousands of years dominated the fertile heart of Asia Minor, living and writing mighty volumes of world art and world history. They that once "came down like a wolf on the fold" are themselves today scattered Christian sheep, harried by their fierce neighbors.

These present Assyrians, largely mixed with the blood of the captive Tribes, represent the oldest existing Christian Church. Their bishops claim an unbroken succession stretching back practically to the time of Jesus. Their Gospel text dates from the second century, nearly two hundred years closer to the event than the Greek MSS. on which our version is based, and free from that translation into a foreign idiom which proverbially destroys the integrity of the written word.

Their native tongue, alone of all spoken now, is that Aramaic Jesus spoke. They still live and think and talk as did the people among whom Jesus was born and to whom he revealed his message.

Mr. Lamsa grew up and was trained for the priesthood amid these unchanged ancient customs and traditions.

From this background of a peculiar intimacy, and with tireless study of the neglected old Aramaic MSS., the author has drawn a portrait of Jesus through native eyes, bringing fresh illumination on many points to Western readers. Again and again dark and troublesome passages, on which commentators have produced libraries of labored explanation, become clear and obvious in the light of the colloquial speech, which the writer knows as only a native knows a language, and the local Oriental habits of thought of those for whom our Gospels were first recorded.

Strangely enough, considering the vast literature on the subject, this seems to be the first such presentation of the historical Jesus by one who speaks Aramaic.

HENRY WYSHAM LANIER

Introduction

Our Assyrian people belong to a country where ancient customs are sacredly and tenaciously held. Railroads and machinery are unknown. Transportation is by mules, camels and on men's backs. The social order, in respect of simple and hospitable ways, continues as in the days of Jesus. Religion, as then, is still the dominant factor. The only literature known is the Bible and the liturgical books used at the church services. The Gospels in the Aramaic are a source of much inspiration to sustain the faith and to cherish the hope of these people, who are now refugees scattered throughout the hot plains of Mesopotamia without home or country, exposed to persecutions and the privations of poverty.

The Aramaic, according to Old Testament history, is the oldest language. Nearly all Biblical names derive their meanings from it. Abraham was an Assyrian who left Haran to settle in Canaan. Later his son Isaac and his grandson Jacob got their wives from Haran. In this land the majority of Jacob's children were born, after which he returned to Canaan. Aramaic, however, was the language used by them at that time and during their sojourn in Egypt. This same language was spoken by their descendants after the occupation of Canaan under Joshua and through the following centuries, including the Exile and the Return. This continuity of language with inevitable variations extended to the days of Jesus. Aramaic was spoken by him and his disciples and by the Jewish people of Palestine. It continued to be the colloquial and literary language of the Jews until the ninth century, when it was displaced by Arabic owing to the Muhammadan conquest.

This language is simple in style, but its figurative expressions and the different meanings given to certain words often cause confusion. This is especially the experience of those not familiar with the customs of the people. For instance, "God hold you" does not mean God sustain you, but God will condemn you in the day of Judgment. "God has given him a lamp" means God has given him a son to continue the family name after his death. "I and my father are one" means I and my father agree. "I have eaten my body and drunk my blood" means I have worked hard. Then again, specific terms are not generally used. Facts, time and localities are of minor importance to a people, most of whom cannot count beyond one hundred and who do it on their fingers. Such people would hardly know the difference between a thousand and a million except that the latter represents a much larger number. There cannot, therefore, be scientific exactness and accuracy in the modern sense. If this were remembered, what appears to be exaggeration is really a characteristic of symbolical language. There is not the slightest idea of trying to deceive and mislead.

All this is radically unlike the Occidental manner of speech, as I found to my confusion after coming to the United States. Books had given information, for instance, that letters are mailed in boxes on the streets, but this was not clear to an Oriental. Nor did he know the difference between "waste" and "west," for the same Aramaic word is often spelled differently. Letters were at first deposited in boxes marked "waste." It was only after repeated failures to receive answers he discovered that his letters had miscarried. On another occasion the price for room and board was baffling because board was understood as an ironing-board, which was not needed by one who had few clothes to be pressed. These are doubtless trifling incidents, but they convinced me of the difference between knowledge gained from books alone and what is obtained from the actual experiences of life.

These mishaps led to a further discovery of difficulties from the other side. Just as an Oriental who does not know Occidental ways is apt to be misled, so an Occidental who does not have a first-hand knowledge of the Orient is likely to misunderstand its peculiarities of speech and customs. This is especially true of the ancient Orient of the first century A.D. In conversation with Americans it was learned that many of them interpret the sayings of Jesus in a literal sense because their original meanings are not clearly conveyed in the English translations.

Indeed, the early translators of the Gospels had no access to the Aramaic *Peshitto* version of the New Testament. Even if they did possess this text, a limited knowledge of the customs and manners of the Near East at that time prevented their accurate rendering of the idiomatic and symbolical expressions in their native context. It is only in recent times that the Near East has been explored, but it is inherently difficult for a foreigner so to immerse himself in its life as to be able to think and feel as its peoples do. This is no reflection, but simply a matter of fact. It implies that the genius of the Orient cannot be adequately grasped by the Occident, for the same reason that the Occident so often mystifies the Orient.

It would, however, be a serious misfortune if the pellucid and persuasive sayings of Jesus are accepted as paradoxical and contradictory. Even those sayings which are considered difficult and treated as having double meanings are perfectly clear to one who is acquainted with present Aramaic, which is virtually the same as the Aramaic of the first century. Add to this the other fact that the manners and customs are practically the same as they were nineteen hundred years ago. One who was born and who lived to early manhood in such an atmosphere, and whose study of the Gospels has been an absorbing interest from his youth, has surely certain qualifications to interpret these holy writings in their original setting.

The favorable reception given to addresses delivered in various parts of the United States and the interested inquiries from several people, have induced me to offer this selection of interpretations of the life and teachings of Jesus. The translations of passages from the Gospels are direct from the *Peshitto* text.

Our people rightly regard Jesus as a neighbor, who understands them with keen sympathy, who reads their hearts with discerning insight, who meets their needs with the fullness of the divine grace. They think of him, not in theological terms, but as the peerless religious soul and the Saviour of the world.

G. M. L.

I. Nearer to Jesus

For the last twenty centuries the world has thought, spoken and written about Jesus more than any other man.

Nearly all great men who have reached world prominence have influenced the hearts of men and women. They have gone down into history as immortals. Some are worshiped by their followers and admirers. Great kings and emperors, long since dead, are remembered through their power and glory and worldly conquests. Men who once by fortune and character were raised to the rank of deities have sunk to obscurity and oblivion. Gods have been born and grown old, and the form of their worship has become legendary. New shrines have been built and dedicated, and the old ones disowned and demolished. Prophets live through their inspiring literature. Heroes are honored because of their gallant acts.

None has surpassed Jesus and nothing has been able to take him from the hearts of men and women who admire and worship him.

Kings and realms bow in prayer to him and crowns are surmounted with his Cross. The world has never worshiped any other man more than Jesus. In heaven and on earth humanity knows no sweeter name. He has received worship through many forms, yet he never sought worshipers, nor did he ever attempt to inaugurate a new system of worship to supplant that of Judaism. He discounted honors and publicity. He refused to be called Rabbi. He instructed his disciples not to call anyone Master, or to seek high places at feasts and weddings. He wanted nothing from men but to do the will of his Father. He came, not that men should sacrifice to him, but that he might be sacrificed for them.

Think of this scientific age in which we are living. Mystery after mystery is unveiled; secret after secret revealed. Not many centuries ago our earth was thought to be the center of the universe and the most important planet of the cosmos. Sun, moon, and stars were created just to serve it.

Now we have found that the earth is one of the smallest stars lost in one of the corners of the universe. And yet through all these centuries of thinking, discovery and research, the world is still more anxious than ever to gain a better understanding of Jesus, his teachings and his life. All the light which this new age has thrown on science and religion has not been enough to reveal to us the inner side of his life and teachings, nor has it helped to bring him nearer to us. Instead it has created new creeds, built up new sects, and contributed much toward the decline of Christianity.

We know less about Jesus now than his followers did in the first century. Yet he was not a philosopher or a magician. He was born in a humble town of humble parents, reared among a simple people, to whom simplicity and poverty were the highest realities in life, and who never spoke or thought in abstruse ways.

Jesus was inspired by the promises which God had made to the people of his faith: the sacred covenant established with Abraham, Isaac and Jacob. As a patriotic Jew, he cherished the great hope for the fulfilment of this covenant. He preached a gospel with simple words, derived from daily language, illustrated with stories which were common to all—a gospel acceptable only to the poor of his time. He chose simple men as his companions. They were regarded as the outcasts of ignorance by the accepted religious teachers who would not think of training such to be leaders. He, moreover, spoke in parables characteristic of all Oriental teachers, in a manner that these unlearned men and the public could understand and grasp.

The world has, nevertheless, made different portraits of Jesus. Some have transformed his simple gospel into a code of philosophy which only philosophers and theologians can understand, and they have written vast commentaries to explain it. In their thought Jesus was a propounder of abstruse theories. Others have tried to picture him as they think he might have been. Some, in portraying him as God of gods, have shorn him of his humanity. His teachings on life have been interpreted as theological dogmas and mysteries. Others, again, have reduced him to a mere man. We cannot overlook his human personality and his human attributes and at the same time think of him as hungry, thirsty, and dying for us. He surely shared in all that is human. A God born, reared and killed would be no example for us. But he was more than human to his contemporaries and indeed also to us.

Jesus, no doubt, is a mystery and he will never be fully understood. But we needlessly multiply difficulties by taking him out of his Oriental context and thinking of him in terms of modern Occidental Christianity and wholly in the light of our complex social life. The stimulus to our rapid transformation during the past nine hundred years has made us like a clock which moves only forward. We think for the future and forget the past. Our religion and worship have grown side by side with our social and economic life; our churches are organized on the same business principles as our industrial institutions. Our schools, colleges and universities graduate lawyers, doctors and politicians, as well as preachers.

In the olden days prophets were called by God, and religious men were selected only from the ranks which represented the moral concerns of the people. In these modern days, instead of raising ourselves above our material interests, we try to make religion fit our social order. We live in a scientific age with an artificial social order; yet we want miracles like those that happened two thousand years ago, to a people who believed in them and who lived close to nature.

And because they do not happen now, we question their reality in the past. Why do we need miracles in an age of airplanes, radio, and railroads? Why do we need healers, with all our doctors and hospitals? Do our religious geniuses believe in healing? Have they ever really tried it? The fact is that some who have tried it with success have been condemned as fanatics. And yet the healing ministry of Jesus was one of his conspicuous achievements.

It is generally held that Jesus came to a world empty of religion, and taught men in a supernatural manner, by revealing thoughts and imaginations hitherto unknown. But, with our superficial knowledge, we fail to realize that the world was never so ready and prepared for the new Gospel, as in the time of Jesus. Behind Christianity lay the influence and experience of more than three hundred years. All over the civilized world there were religious movements making for common understanding and unification. The existing religions of that time were worn out, corrupt and unpopular. There were schools of religion in Egypt, Greece and Persia. Scholars and philosophers in those countries strove to fashion a universal religion to fit the needs of mankind, regardless of geographical and racial distinction. But their attempts collapsed, leaving only shattered material for their successors.

The amazing fact about Jesus is that he, a simple peasant, free from any political and religious backing, was able to formulate a religion which appealed to the souls of all mankind, and to leave behind an unconquerable influence which still abides and will so abide forever, regardless of all political, social and economic changes throughout the world.

Great prophets, like Moses and Elijah, had preceded him by many centuries. Sacred writings were put into books. Old Eastern cults were dying out and new religions with new messages were taking their places. Schools of learning were engaged in the search for knowledge and salvation. As a conqueror he was preceded by mighty Assyrian, Egyptian, Persian and Greek emperors. As a prophet he succeeded in the direct line of Hebrew seers, who hailed the advent of a Saviour. As a philosopher, he was born four hundred years after Socrates and Plato. Jesus, moreover, came into a world ruled by a great empire which had established peace and order, whose military organization and institutions were not equaled by any other nation until the beginning of the twentieth century, and whose laws have become the laws of the world.

Some have forgotten the past and think that Jesus came like a prince into a world where everything was prepared for him, with a program and itinerary well planned in advance. On the contrary, he entered upon his ministry with little or no publicity. He was mostly unknown or misknown. He labored within a limited circle and finally met with a malefactor's death.

Our present attempt is to take Jesus back where he was when he lived on earth, to interpret his sayings from the Aramaic language which he spoke, and to consider the answers he gave to the questions asked him, in their original form. We might understand him better when we approach him from the standpoint of the people of his race and time. Such a procedure is practicable because the social customs and manners in Assyria have virtually remained unchanged from ancient times. The chief reason for this is the isolation of the Assyrians, due to the militant power of their Islamic rulers.

The contemporary misconception of the Scriptures has led many to think of Jesus as more severe and fanatic in his interpretation of the law than the scribes who thought and reasoned literally, and who were condemned by him for doing so. For instance, men were told to cut off their right arm and to pluck out their right eye if these caused them to sin. Rich men were barred from entering into the Kingdom of Heaven. A little faith would remove mountains; yet neither Jesus nor his disciples changed one of the smallest hills in Judæa. He did not permit any, even his disciples, to pluck out their eyes. Nor did Peter cut off his arm when it offended him at Gethsemane. These statements sound harsh to an American, but they are clear to one familiar with the manner of Aramaic speech. The disciples and others to whom these words were addressed did not question them because they understood their meaning.

Consider again what Jesus said about divorce and *Shvikta*, that is, women who were arbitrarily driven out from their homes by their husbands. He told his disciples that men were not to put away their wives, except for adultery. They were surprised and exclaimed: "If there is so much difficulty between a man and his wife, it is not worth while to marry." Jesus explained: "This saying does not apply to every man, but to whom it is needed. For there are eunuchs who were born this way from their mothers' wombs, and there are eunuchs who have been made eunuchs by men, and there are eunuchs who have made themselves eunuchs for the sake of the Kingdom of Heaven. To him who can grasp, this is enough." What he meant was that there are other causes for divorce besides adultery; that women can also divorce their husbands if sexually unfit; that a man who had been made an eunuch and married can divorce his wife without accusing her of adultery, as is often done in the East; that a man who married an undivorced woman, whose husband had put her out of his house, commits adultery. Indeed, this frank way of upholding and protecting the personal purity and social rights of women was never done before in all the religious history of the Orient. It is this fact which has given Jesus so strong a hold on the womanhood of the world, for even Muhammadan women today adore and love him.

II. God Our Father

The Jews, though a humble race, often defeated by their enemies and at times carried into captivity and humiliated, boasted in their pride that they were free sons of Abraham. As a race they had little to be proud of except their unseen God and their sacred worship—discovered by Abraham, shaped by Moses and the prophets, but now corrupted by the traditions of the elders. Their father Abraham was only a servant of the God whom they so mysteriously worshiped.

Jewish traditional ancestry, so sacredly kept by every loyal and patriotic Jew, did not appeal to Jesus. The God of heaven, as conceived by the priests, was only an overlord, a jealous god, hungry and thirsty for sacrificial meat and the blood of animals. The Hebrew God in olden times had cared for his people, freed them from slavery, guided them through the wilderness to the promised land. Now it seemed that he depended as much on his people as in the past they had depended on him. Even his ethical standards were not much higher than those of the pagan gods whom the Jews despised. Jahveh, moreover, in selecting his sacrifices, was more concerned in receiving sacrifices than in restoring the soul of the worshiper. He was more jealous of his glory than of the welfare of his people. He was the father of the Jewish nation, not to love and care for the members of his race, but to be loved and served by them.

The pomp of ceremony attached to the mystic worship of the war-lord of Israel was indeed alien to Jesus' conception of God. To the Jews prayer had become a duty, religion a function, and the loving father a tyrannical ruler. The dogmas and traditions of the elders and the corrupt sacrificial system inaugurated by the professionalized priesthood had for centuries created a well-founded deistic conception of God. The creator of earth and mankind seemed to have nothing to do with his children; his only approach was through sacrifices and priestly mediums. Salvation of men depended on their obedience to the state law, and religion was thus joined to the State. Jahveh was supreme ruler over both, but men were trained to pledge their allegiance first to the traditions of the priests. In reality, the God of Israel was less a father than a pagan god, alert only to reward his worshipers. Invariably the pagan deities presided over fertile agricultural lands. They were supposed to bring prosperity and shower blessings on their adherents. In this respect they outshone Jahveh, who seemed to be always in want, inclined to be more destructive than constructive, a seeker of vengeance instead of a forgiver of human frailty.

The true conception of God—Father—as revealed to Jesus was gained not so much from knowledge of the Scriptures as from experiences of his early youth. He had seen shepherds searching after water and grass for their sheep. The shepherds so loved their sheep that they would risk their lives for them. Not so was it with hired shepherds who thought more of their pay than of the real welfare of their flocks. Human fathers loved their children. How much more would the heavenly Father, source of eternal love, do for his children without any thought of reward!

An Easterner often addresses his guest or his servant as "my father." To call a man father is the highest honor one can bestow on another. Nevertheless, every Easterner is proud of his actual father and his ancestors. "I am son of my father; I will do what he commands," an Assyrian will say. There is nothing more dear to him than his traditional family ties. On the other hand, if the relationship on the maternal side is more important than that of the paternal, or if the father died while his family were young, children are usually called sons of their mothers. For instance, Joab was known as the son of Zeruiah, and Jesus was called "the son of Mary."

Jesus also used the name *Barnasha*—"son of man." This term is used by Aramaic-speaking people to refer to mankind in general or to an individual male, or to one whose identity is not known, or to distinguish human beings from the animal creation.

It is supposed that Joseph had died when Jesus was a little over twelve. Nothing is said in the Gospels concerning Joseph after his return from Jerusalem, when Jesus was taken to be presented to God at the temple. On the other hand, the mother and brothers of Jesus are often mentioned. During the years when he advanced in age and wisdom he forgot his earthly father.

Born into a peasant family, reared in the little obscure village of Nazareth, Jesus had nothing to boast about in the ancestry of Joseph. He was merely a carpenter who did little odd jobs in town, an occupation despised by an Easterner. His ancestors were termed by the Jews, invaders who came from Assyria, whose claim to the Jewish race was strongly repudiated by Zerubbabel and the elders centuries before. Other men often talked about their fathers, for their families in the past had belonged to the nobility.

An Eastern father generally takes sides with his son, whether his son is right or wrong, when quarreling with other young men. Jesus had no one to fight for him, or to avenge his wrongs. Even though a young man be without a father, at times he is protected, for some of the kindly Eastern men would not treat an orphan boy unjustly. They often say, "Do not hit him; his father is dead." In the East an orphan is known as God's child. Jesus relied on no one but the unseen universal Father who was revealed to him as the only source of help. His faith in God as a protector became stronger and more vital, while dreams of his earthly father vanished. Gentle and meek in his manner, men and women called him "Son of God," in Aramaic, *Bar-alaha*. This is the name which the Aramaic-speaking people give a meek young man. An older man is called "Man of God," *Nasha d'alaha*. Jesus is now so close to his heavenly Father that he instructs his followers not to call anyone father—"One is your Father in heaven."

In the East it is not unusual to call God "my Father" and to name men "sons of God." God called David, Solomon and Cyrus "my sons." David exhorted Solomon to look to God as his father. The expression "My father and I are one" means: "What I am doing is the will of my father. My father would do the same; we are of one accord."

Jesus thus revealed the God of Israel, not only as the Father of Abraham, Isaac, Jacob, and the Jews, but also as the Father of Galileans, Gentiles and sinners, who is more glad to see one sinner repent than ninety-nine righteous men. The God of the universe can be worshiped not only in Jerusalem and Samaria, but everywhere. "God is a Spirit, and they that worship him must worship him in spirit and in truth," said Jesus when conversing with the woman of Samaria.

In his revelation of the universal father Jesus

discarded all magical ceremonies, sacrifices, temples, and long prayers. The Father of Jesus is father of all men. He can be approached only through a shorter and simpler prayer addressed to "Our universal Father." This prayer given by Jesus in Aramaic is still used every day, in its original form, by the Assyrian people:

Avon dvashmaya nithkadash shmakh: taty malcothakh: nehwey sevianakh aicanna dvashmaya op barah. Havlan lakhma dsonkanan yomana: washboklan khoben: aicanna dop khnan shbakn lkhayaven. Oola talan lnisuna ella passan min bisha: mittol ddilakhye malcotha okhela ootishbokhta: lalam almin: Amen.

III. The Healer

The wandering Nazarene who a short time before had been denounced, condemned, and expelled as a dangerous dreamer and heretic by the synagogue at Nazareth, and deserted even by his own people, was now different. He found favor with God and men. He discovered that he was no longer Jesus of Nazareth; no more the shepherd and carpenter; no longer the son of Joseph and Mary. He was Christ, the Son of the Living God; not of this world, but of the other world. The secrets of nature were no longer hidden from him. The thoughts of material possessions had disappeared from his mind. The barrier which separated this earth from heaven had vanished. He was not afraid of criticism and hostility. His love for suffering humanity had made him forget his parents: "Who is my mother and brothers?"

The man who had failed to satisfy the people of Nazareth, as a carpenter and successor to his father, had become a popular orator throughout his country. He had never studied philosophy, but he became a master logician. There were no more doubts in his mind; no desires to tempt his God. The Sermon on the Mount had won public admiration for him. Sympathy on the part of those who heard him had taken the place of hatred; admiration had replaced insults. The broken hearts of his countrymen were comforted. A new way of salvation for men was found. The law which Moses had inscribed on hard granite tablets was to be written into the hearts of human beings. The secrets of the sacred books which prophets and priests had kept from the people were to be exposed. The bodies and minds of those afflicted were to be healed. Men who were sick and sinners were to be trained as healers of humanity. The ignorant fishermen, who were hitherto not allowed even to touch the sacred books, were instructed to explain correctly the law and the prophets.

A new chapter in the history of religion was about to be written, which summed up law and prophecy. The God who hitherto had revealed himself only through prophets was to approach even the most humble. What a victory for an obscure preacher who had sprung from poverty into notoriety and prominence, and who fearlessly denounced the Pharisees and priests! "Verily, I say unto you, that the publicans and the harlots go into the kingdom of God before you."

Jesus was not afraid of breaking the Sabbath, the most sacred institution in Jewish religion. In his teachings he did not enjoin a strict observance of the law. He had no ties with any organization which would block his way or hinder his progress. Without publicity and the assurance for a living, Jesus entered upon his career relying on God. He spoke for God, but with authority. It was not so much what the Scriptures said but what he declared that the Scriptures meant.

His popularity increased every day. His persuasive power of speech attracted the multitudes. Instead of seeking men to hear him, he drew away from the crowds. The lonely preacher of Nazareth, who had hitherto addressed only groups of beggars, unhired laborers, boys who had come to hear him for fun, was now beset by eager crowds. The more they knew him, the less he revealed himself to them. He showed no pride in his speeches or in his healing power. After long, weary and tiresome preaching hours, instead of taking a good offering and retiring to the more healthy places in town, he went to a cave for rest. A few fish and a few dry loaves of bread given by some kind friend were sufficient for his needs, with a little cave for his bed and a stone for his pillow.

A poor workingman among the poor, a countryman preaching among the country people, Jesus drew people from all walks of life. His power was a strong wind spreading his fame abroad. It brought even representatives of the capital city to question him. "By what power are you doing these things?" they asked him. "You have no connection with the priestly system in Jerusalem. You are not even a rabbi, not even a good Jew. Tell us by what authority you do these things. Under what God are you working? Who commissioned you to preach and heal?"

It was needless for Jesus to argue all these points. They would not have believed him if he told them he was authorized by their God. They asked him for a sign, and he replied: "If you will tell me from where the baptism of John came, from heaven or from earth, I will tell you by what authority I do these things." They were afraid to answer; for they believed that John was a prophet, though when John was alive they did not believe in him. "He is healing in the name of the chief of the devils," said some of the Jews. "We know there are evil spirits which have power to heal, and which can bestow gifts upon their followers. This man is a Samaritan. He is doing these things in the name of Baal-Zebub, the head of devils and god of Ekron."

Jesus could no longer hold his peace. He could forgive them, but he could not remain silent before such an insult. "If a man blaspheme against the Father, his sins will be forgiven, or if he blaspheme against the Son, his sins will be forgiven. But whosoever blaspheme against the Holy Spirit, his sins shall never be forgiven in this world and in the world to come."

The Aramaic word *rokha* means spirit, the healing power, not God or the Holy Ghost. *Rokha* is the spirit of God the Easterners invoke to cure their diseases. It is the spirit that passes from the healer to the sick, the spirit which speaks through the prophets. This is what Elisha sought in that memorable meeting with Elijah. "And it came to pass, when they were gone over, that Elijah said unto Elisha, ask what I shall do for thee, before I be taken away from thee. And

Elisha said, I pray thee, let a double portion of thy spirit be upon me." This word *rokha* also means wind, pride, temper and rheumatism, although the English translators have invariably rendered the word as spirit or Holy Ghost. For instance, the familiar beatitude should be translated, "Blessed are the poor in pride"; the man with the evil spirit often means the man with a hot temper; the woman, suffering from the spirit of infirmity for twelve years and bent down in consequence, was afflicted with rheumatism, according to the Aramaic version of Luke's Gospel.

The blind teachers of the law understood what Jesus meant, but they doubted that he was invoking the Holy Spirit in his healing acts. It was a rebuke, in reply to their false accusations. "If you speak against God he will forgive you, because you have not seen him and you do not know him. If you speak against me, I will forgive you, for you do not know where I come from. You are of this world; but I am of the other world. How can you be forgiven when you see with your eyes devils cast out, the eyes of the blind opened, the sick healed and say these are by the devil? Will the spirit of the devil heal the sick? Can the devil work against himself? Can a kingdom be divided against itself, and survive?"

The people who followed him were not only sick in body, but in heart and mind. Words without works would have meant nothing to them, as the hot stones meant nothing to him when he was hungry in the desert. If he could win their hearts, why not speak a word of comfort to heal their bodies? If a word could transform a man into a new life, why could it not create a new body? One who can heal souls, can also heal bodies. When the soul is well the mind is at peace and the body is healthy.

Jesus lived in a land where nothing was new and nothing had grown old. The inhabitants of Judaea and Galilee believed in spiritual healing. They had no medical schools and doctors, but spiritual healers rose from time to time. Their early ancestors, the Assyrians and Babylonians, were astronomers, philosophers and magicians. The men who had tried to build a tower to fight with God had also searched the earth and sought the help of heavenly bodies to prevent sickness and death, and to live forever. Their pagan religions had magical forms of healing.

There was nothing which had not been tried for the cure of bodies. Drinking the water from certain springs and resting in the shade of isolated trees were the only medicine for certain diseases, such as fever and leprosy. The sacred trees had comforted weary travelers, restored those who had sought refuge under their refreshing branches, and healed those suffering from fever. Under their healing boughs famous holy men had lived. The springs likewise gave new life to weary desert travelers. These healers were using nature against nature. There were seers and practitioners of black magic, who put the body above the spirit, and who disputed the validity of material forms. The Galileans were believers in devils and demons, the unseen spirits whom most men did not know how to worship.

Disease played havoc with the Palestinians because of their little knowledge of hygiene. In a country where water was scarce and bathing unknown, the people were subject to skin diseases, troubles from empty stomachs and from overeating and drinking during weddings and feasts. Internal troubles were not understood at that time nor do the Easterners understand them today. Even those who were not sick sought Jesus' help to prevent them from contagious diseases. To some he recommended fasting, to others, prayer, communing with the Divine Spirit.

Some were sick in mind; others were terrified by the thought that they had contracted diseases.

The lepers, the blind, the outcasts, made up his early audiences. Most of them cared little about what he said. They had come only to be healed. They had been to other healers and had tried remedies of every kind; and they were ready to go to anyone who could cure their bodies.

Jesus soon found he must minister to the bodies as well as to the souls, the body being just as important as the soul. The soul cannot be seen without a body, nor can the body exist without a soul. Prophets had healed the sick, cleansed the lepers, raised the dead. Why not he? Is the Messiah less than a prophet? Even in obscure towns healers were speaking words of comfort to the sick and dying. Why not he? He expected nothing from those who sought his help, hence he would not be embarrassed by their seeking him. He was under no obligation except that of love. He had received freely. He gave freely. He authorized no publicity which would commercialize his healing power. He never recommended medicines; a few simple remarks were enough: "If ye believe, thy faith has healed thee. If you be trustworthy, you will receive."

His work of healing brought fame and made friends for him; it also brought disappointments and aroused enemies. At times out of hundreds of sick persons who were brought to him only a few were healed, those who had faith in him. Others whose bodies were not cured left the place cursing and shouting insults. He taxed his powers of endurance by sympathizing with the afflicted. He would never try to heal if they left him alone. He had never boasted of this power. He never pretended that he was the only healer in the world. When his disciples failed to heal a sick man he told them, "If you have faith as a mustard seed you can remove mountains. No magic, no tricks, just a little faith. Any one of you can do it."

Easterners were accustomed to the long prayers, incantations, charms, and the magic of healers who perverted spiritual healing into a profitable profession. Men and women often went away disappointed because the words uttered by Jesus were too simple and not like the magical ejaculations and complicated prescriptions of professional healers. He had no drums with which to chase away evil spirits; no charcoal to blacken faces; no snakes to frighten those who had fever. His were only words as soft as spring winds, and as free to those who came to him. Occasionally some who were not satisfied with mere words begged for a formula. He smiled at them. He knew they were simple-minded country folk. They understood things materially and literally. He often granted their request. Instead of prescribing water from seven springs, soil from seven roads that never cross each other and that are only traversed by virgins, he took a little earth and spat on it, then placed it on the place which was to be healed. To the sufferer he said, "Your sins are forgiven; do not tell it to anyone."

"Tell no one" is an Aramaism which means, "Go and tell everybody." It could not have been otherwise, for the healing works of Jesus were mostly done in the midst of crowded throngs. In the East the things which are told in confidence are preached from the house tops. There is no other way by which news may be spread so rapidly as by disclosing a secret with the instructions, "Tell to no one." "What I tell you secretly, tell it openly, and what you hear through your ears, preach from the house tops."

Among those who came to seek his help were many who had evil spirits. The Aramaic word for evil spirits is *shedy*. The term is used of those who talk too much or who are demented. Jesus was often called *shedana*, which means crazy, because he said certain things that no one understood; not even the men whom he was training knew the meaning of some of his remarks.

Among those who came to him were the doubting, under bondage of sin, and the weak-minded. They were not able to think straight or speak logically. Their minds were disarranged and hungry for the truth. Some spoke too much and said nothing. When they faced Jesus and looked into his calm face and heard his persuasive words, they found something wrong with themselves. It is the power which radiates from the personality of the healer that cures the sick. Personality is the magnetic instrument through which the divine power passes. The healer is the medium through whose personality the divine power manifests itself. Any doubt in his mind will obstruct the passage of the healing spirit, just as rust between two connecting wires interrupts the electric current. Jesus knew by one look into the faces of men and women the inner part of their lives.

The men who argued with rabbis and who did not believe in the Scriptures began to realize they lacked understanding. His logic of common sense made them marvel. His sharp accusations of religious leaders pleased them. These men who despised religious reformers, with whom the rabbis could not agree, and whom they could not persuade to join their congregations, were termed by other Jews "possessed with devils." They loved and admired Jesus because he denounced the religion of formality. They called him Christ, Son of the Living God. Humanity could not build this character and produce this type of holy man. Human tongue could not speak with this amazing power. They saw God in him. Who else could he be but the Son of the Living God?

One afternoon when Jesus had finished preaching he went to the house of Peter at Capernaum, a small fishing town near the lake. Peter's wife was absent, and his mother-in-law happened to be sick with fever. In the East fever is not considered a serious sickness. Men and women stricken with fever do not cease their labors; they harvest, milk, care for sheep, cook, and do every kind of work. When there is no work to be done, some prefer sleeping to walking under the heat of the sun.

The sound of feet and the conversation of guests, as Peter led them into the narrow alley, excited the sick woman thus awakened from her sleep. There was no one in the house to entertain an unexpected and popular guest, the Master of her son-in-law. Jesus entered and stood beside the sick bed, gazing at the woman. At the sight of Jesus' face she could no longer rest under the covers. She could not see such an honorable guest waiting in the house with nothing prepared for him. The unexpected coming of Jesus made her forget she was sick. She lost every thought of herself and her mind was occupied solely with the presence of the beloved guest whom her humble son-in-law had brought to the house. She rose up quickly and began preparing food.

An Eastern man would feel embarrassed if he had to cook and serve food in the absence or illness of the women members of his family. That is a woman's work; therefore, the woman who had been ill for weeks was now walking in the streets, hurrying from house to house, borrowing bread, eggs, and plates. She suddenly realized that there were more important things than herself and the fever. She had always desired to see the Teacher of her son-in-law in her home. Excited and occupied as she was, she had no time to think about her fever. Her hands were busy preparing food, her ears were listening to the words which flowed so graciously from the mouth of the new Prophet. Her fever left her and she was healed.

IV. A Test Case

One day, while Jesus was resting in the house of one of his friends, a group of professional reformers came in and brought to him a woman who was taken in adultery. According to Aramaic speech, that means a woman found to be pregnant. A woman can commit adultery, and as long as she is not found with child she cannot be accused. In the East the committing of adultery is unusual and seldom happens. This woman's accusers were not much concerned with her conduct. What they wanted was to test Jesus' attitude towards morality. They had often talked about Jesus, and had frequently accused him of being the friend of sinners, in association with women of bad reputation, and a prophet who had no respect for law and decency.

A TEST CASE

If this woman had been actually caught committing adultery on that day, the man who had sinned with her would also have been brought to the place of accusation. According to Mosaic law the man shares responsibility with the woman, and both are stoned. "Rabbi, what shall we do with this woman?" they asked Jesus. "According to the law of Moses, she must be stoned. What do you say about her?"

The woman was known as an adulteress in the town. Most of her accusers knew her well; doubtless they had themselves committed adultery with her. They could lay their hands on her any time they pleased. If these men had wanted to punish her, they could have taken her to the priests, as the latter had the sole power to condemn her. The priests still maintained the freedom of the Mosaic law under Roman rule, but if they could not condemn her to death, how could a Galilean, not even accepted as a Jew, condemn her? If he had recommended that she be put to death, they would have stoned her and placed the responsibility on him. Jesus would then have had to answer to Jewish and Roman authorities. If he had said that adultery was not a crime and could not be punished, then they would have accused him of being in sympathy with sinners.

While these men conversed with one another, at times stroking their beards and occasionally blaming the rabbis for not enforcing the law, Jesus sat still, looking at the ground. He listened to the men who sat around him in a circle, and who were apparently unashamed at the embarrassing situation. They were playing the part of professional reformers and trying to enforce a law which they themselves had never obeyed.

Jesus listened to their accusations. He knew what they had to say before they opened their mouths. He knew why they had come. He knew that some of them were as guilty as the woman in their midst. They could not look into his face, so he was unable to see their expressions. Once in a while he glanced at the hypocritical countenances. Then again he looked at the ground, his fourth finger making geometrical lines and crossing them in the form of a chessboard.

Jesus was carefully considering what judgment to pass. The penalty under Mosaic law was mandatory; the punishment was death. But to Jesus' mind adultery was only one of the sins. The woman had broken only one of the sacred Commandments; her accusers had broken many. Jesus did not write on the ground, nor could the people have read the writing on the earth if he had written. Customarily, Easterners, when confronted by a serious problem, begin scratching the ground. Some of them use a stick instead of the finger. They do it even if they sit on a carpet. In most places, however, where the Eastern customs have not changed, there is no carpet. Meetings are held on the ground in the house, or outside on the roof.

After the long presentations and argumentary debates, everyone was silent. The pretense of sincerity by this woman's accusers, in defending the moral law, was so obvious that they could no longer carry on conversation. The interview was over. Jesus then lifted his hand from the ground and for a moment silently scrutinized their faces. Again with eyes fixed downward, he began to speak. His answer was brief: "Let anyone of you who is without sin cast the first stone."

The accusers immediately realized that they themselves were guilty, and that if the woman should be stoned for her misconduct by some of the men who had gathered there and who were innocent, they themselves would be stoned with her. Moreover, they perceived that Jesus knew their inner secrets. They were afraid; they began to leave the house one by one. The woman was left alone.

When Jesus saw that all of her accusers had left and that none of them had dared cast a stone at the woman whom they had tried to condemn, he turned his face to her: "Where are those thine accusers? Hath no man condemned thee?" She said, "No man, Lord." And Jesus said, "Neither do I condemn thee: Go, and sin no more."

V. The Courageous Challenge

> "Do not accumulate gold, nor silver, nor brass in your purses, nor a bag for your journey, nor two shirts, nor shoes, nor a walking-stick, for a workman is at least worthy of his food."

Gold is the soul of the material world and the god of this earth. For unknown ages this precious metal has exerted a tremendous influence in the political and economic life of the world, and for it humanity has fought its historic battles. Money has also gained control in the realm of spirit. Priests and merchants have coveted it; high priests have loved it more than God. Even religious men have used every conceivable method to acquire it. Gold and silver can buy honors, raise men from obscurity into prominence, change servants into masters, make farmers doctors of philosophy, and shoemakers presidents. Moreover, sins can be "forgiven" by money. High religious and governmental offices can be sold and bought. It can also bless, heal, and curse. There are few things that mortals cannot purchase with the power of money.

Nevertheless, to Jesus, gold and silver which men loved so much were not more precious than soil and water which contained life. These two scarce and precious metals God had created for the use of men, to be made into spoons, cups, plates, and ornaments of beauty. They were not intended to be buried in treasuries and bank vaults. Indeed, savage peoples have so used them, but civilized nations have always worshiped them.

"What is the use if a man gain the whole world, but lose his soul?" What can be bought with gold can be sold for more gold. What money can build money can destroy. The Jewish temple was often ransacked and destroyed for the sake of its rich gold treasures. The knowledge that abundant wealth, which Jewish kings and priests had collected from their people, was stored in the luxurious temple brought the influx of Assyrian and Chaldean armies into Judæa.

Moreover, Judaism became weakened and corrupted by the rival rulers and high priests, who bitterly fought each other to acquire high offices which yielded more money. The solid gold vases and temple ornaments did not help to better the worshipers. Instead, the holy golden altars and the rich temple treasures made them proud and overbearing.

The new message to humanity, proclaimed by the strange Prophet, required neither temples, high priests, nor treasures. His teachings could not be blended with the old system. The old sheepskins could not hold the new wine. Men were now to be mobilized, to enlist in the service of the new kingdom without wages and honors, and to be asked to leave not only their earthly possessions, but their wives and children. The preachers of the new Gospel were to give their lives, if need be, for its sake. They were not to look behind in order to see how much was accomplished, or complain of heavy burdens. "No man, having put his hand to the plow, and looking back, is fit for the kingdom of God." In the East a servant who, while plowing, looks behind him to see how much he has accomplished, is considered an inefficient worker; while the best worker is the servant who looks constantly to the unplowed ground ahead of him.

Jesus did not hate money of itself, but he despised the lust and usage of it. If the sacred temple money derived from good-will offerings had corrupted the priests of his Father, why should it not corrupt his own disciples? Indeed, the Jews loved their God and gave liberally to worship him; they were willing to die for their religion, but most of their priests loved only money. Jesus well knew the methods by which it was extracted from the poor, only to be hoarded by the priests and government officials. He had heard priests loudly blessing those who gave liberally and murmuring when the poor dropped small copper coins. Once in the temple he noticed a poor old woman, bent from overwork, walking slowly and dropping in the alms-basin two of the smallest temple coins, the only money she had. It meant depriving herself of bread and clothing in order to part with it; but the priest in charge of alms was not satisfied. He did not even look at this poor woman or trouble himself to say a few comforting words to her for the generous contribution. But Jesus commended her sacrifice.

His followers were recruited from the ranks of the poor people. They had never seen the shiny yellow metal except when they were in the temple. They were, therefore, more likely to become greedy and victims to the temptation of riches. When a poor man suddenly acquires wealth he generally becomes like a horse without reins. Jesus wanted his disciples to be free from this burden and simple in their living. Without gold or silver they would travel as free men in the wide world.

If men who came to them were not healed, the disciples were not to be embarrassed. They had not taken anything from the sick ones and it was not their fault if these were not restored to health. On the other hand, some of the shrewd Jews and Syrians expected to harvest where they had not sown. They expected things gratis. What would happen if they paid for healing and were not healed?

In the East a traveler is killed only when the bandits find money in his purse. This is done that the identity of the murderers may not be revealed. One traveling without money has nothing to fear. If he is met by robbers they may offer to help and let him go in peace. Some highwaymen, not without the virtue of hospitality, usually share their scanty supplies of food with travelers whom they meet, and in return relieve them of their shoes, clothes, or other articles.

In Syria, Palestine, as well as in other parts of the East, robbery and banditry are profitable occupations and in most cities are honorable pursuits. Curiously enough, many bandits hold high religious offices; some are looked upon as saints. When they die, shrines are built over their graves. They pray, fast, and give alms to the poor more abundantly than the men who steal and cheat under the guise of temple religion. Indeed, Eastern robbers and bandits are as much in business as merchants and industrialists.

Jesus knew that his disciples would receive abundant gifts for healing. They would be honored by their admirers with rich clothes, shoes, and other priceless presents. Many would give all their wealth for the sake of having their bodies healed, their sight restored, or their loved ones raised from the dead. The possession of wealth was soon to stir rivalries and hatreds which would weaken their ranks and impair the progress of their work. Some of the disciples would repudiate those who healed in their territory, claiming that only to them had the Lord intrusted the power of healing. Spiritual healing would be commercialized and dominated by mercenary men, who in turn would pervert it into witchcraft for the sake of worldly gains. They were to fall the victims of professional highwaymen who would kidnap them for ransom.

Their Master showed them a better way and set an example for them to follow. These simple peasants were to go as sheep among wolves; they were to be hated, persecuted, and killed for what they preached. "The disciple is not above his master, nor the servant above his lord." His enemies had insulted, hated, and even tried to stone him; they must not expect different treatment.

Jesus taught that there is no better weapon with which his men could conquer the world than the sheer force of sincerity and humility. The power of the Word of God was to combat the power of money. Great emperors and military geniuses who had attempted to conquer nations had gone down in defeat. Wealth had failed to make a better world. The prayers and supplications of the high priests had ascended no higher than their golden altars.

According to this new program, money could not make saints out of sinners. Sacrifices could not yield forgiveness. God as revealed by Jesus was to take care of those who labored for the cause of his Kingdom. Jesus' disciples were to preach freely, heal freely, and live freely. They were to teach the world the folly of worldliness and graft. They were to change the hearts of those who worshiped wealth. They themselves must have one shirt, in order to be able to tell others to give their extra shirts away.

These men who had left a few old nets with little hesitancy and followed him were soon to leave their wives and children and lay down their lives for the Gospel's sake. "If any man come to me, and hate not[1] his father, and mother, and wife, and children, and brethren, and sisters, yea, and his own life also, he cannot be my disciple." His disciples were not even to permit men to call them master; they were not to sit at the head at banquets and feasts. They were to be content with one shirt, a pair of sandals, and with what people offered them for food. They were to rely on God for their safety, and on the generosity of their fellow men for their maintenance.

The workers are worthy of their food, if not worthy of their hire. The Aramaic *sebarta* means food. In the East an inefficient laborer is only hired for what he eats. Food as the price of labor has never been disputed in Eastern coun-

---

[1] The word *saney* in Aramaic means remove to one side, and hence hate here has the idea of a lower preference in comparison with the demands of the Gospel.

tries. Whether a laborer is good or not, he is employed to work only for his food. The glad tidings which these men were to preach to their fellow men, if not worth gold or silver, were certainly deserving of a few loaves of bread and cheese, a few figs and raisins. What else would the country people offer a stranger?

The hospitality of the Eastern peoples exceeds all their other virtues. The stranger who unexpectedly enters a house not only expects free lodging, but also comforts for his tired feet. When the greetings of a traveling-man are received by the master of the house, the women immediately rush to take his shoes from his feet. A young girl will hurry to bring cold water to wash his feet. He is made to feel as though he were in his own home, and he is expected to stay in that house as long as he is in town. As a mark of genuine hospitality an Eastern guest is asked as often as seven times to eat. The guest refuses by saying "Thank you. I have just eaten. I am not hungry." But the host insists by holding on to his garment and urging him, saying, "By God and his Holy Scriptures, you must eat." This is the custom to which Jesus referred in the parable about compelling guests to attend.

There are times when a guest is not welcome

and the men of the house do not rise before him. The same words are used by guest and host in greeting each other. The guest's greeting of "peace" is returned to him in such a cold manner that he immediately understands he is not welcome. The same discourtesy might be repeated in other houses. The weary and discouraged stranger then loosens the straps of his sandals and shakes the sand out. When this is done near the entrance of the house, it signifies that the house has broken the code of hospitality. The dust becomes a witness. The tired and dusty traveler will even refuse to quench his thirst in that house.

La tshalamon lamdinata dbeth Israel damma dnetey brey dnasha: "You shall not yet finish converting all the cities of the house of Israel until the Son of man shall come back." The fields are white, and the harvest is plenty, but reapers are few. The disciples were to work to the end. First among their own people, then among the pagans. It was a hard task, a new career for men who never had spoken in public, who had never dared to protest when treated unjustly by state officials. Now they were to stand before governors and kings. The Spirit was to teach them what to say. Their work would progress slowly. They were to meet opposition, but they were to march forward. They would not finish converting the cities of Israel until Jesus would return on the last day. *Amen amarna lkhon dla tebar sharbta hadey damma dhalen koolhen nevian:* "Truly I say unto you, that this generation [tribe] shall not discontinue until all of these happen." The Jewish race was to continue to the last day. It will be the last to be converted. But this work of evangelization of all peoples was to be continued for centuries, despite opposition and persecution.

VI. True Treasure

"Do not lay for yourselves treasures in the ground, a place where rust and moth destroy, and where thieves break through and steal. But lay for yourselves a treasure in heaven, where neither rust nor moth destroy, and where thieves do not break through and steal: For where your treasure is, there is your heart also."

Burying treasures in the ground is the safest way one can keep his money in the East. This custom was adopted thousands of years ago and is carried on today in most of the Eastern countries without the slightest modification.

Owing to robberies, revolutions, and continuous wars, Easterners have been content with the "burying" system instead of using banks, bonds, and trust companies. Buried money might be safe from fluctuation and bankruptcy, but not from thieves. Although stealing from houses is considered a sin, stealing from fields and localities outside of the house is lawful. Thus, while some men bury their gold and silver, others hunt to find treasure.

Family savings are buried in the fields or under rocks or furtively hidden in the walls of the house. No one knows where the money is concealed except the man who at night buried his treasure. He does not even tell his own wife and children. Generally, men who bury their money take oath that they have none. "I swear by God I have no money or treasure. You can search my field if you wish. If I had money I would buy shoes for my wife." This is done to escape loaning to friends and relatives who cannot pay back. If the money is discovered the owner then cannot claim it, and the finder becomes the legal possessor of the treasure trove. In cases of sudden death, the hoard is lost forever.

Gold-hunters through experience and continued search learn the deepest secrets of these hiders. Whenever they see a sign that gives the slightest indication of a treasure, they start a search.

Therefore, those whose money is buried in the ground away from their home cannot sleep well. Frequently they pass near the place where their savings are buried, to see if robbers have discovered them or made any excavation near the place. Their thoughts, day and night, are buried in the ground with their money. If they happen to dream of something relating to the loss of money, they get up at night to see if the treasure is safe. With their wealth their happiness and religious life also lie buried.

Jesus in his early youth knew men and boys who customarily went out on these treasure hunts. In the East there has never been a law to prevent men from seeking the buried wealth of others. Whatever a man finds is his. If he happens to find it in a field belonging to another, he hastens to buy that field or tries to steal the buried money at night. Often there is fighting for the possession of certain places where money is supposed to be. Jesus had watched men working in the fields, and suspected them of burying their money.

This wealth could have been loaned to those who were in need; but the greed of these men exceeded all their virtues. Jesus considered money a blessing to those who use it for a good purpose; a curse to those who worship it. Abundant natural resources were created for the use of men, not for one man, but for all men. God and nature cannot be fooled. What difference does it make whether the gold is stored as secret treasure or buried in the depths of a mountain? The material is there.

"No man can serve two masters, for either he will hate the one and be friendly to the other, or he may honor one and despise the other. You cannot serve God and worldly things. Therefore I say to you, Do not worry yourself as to what you will eat and what you will drink, or, for your body, what you will wear. Is not life more important than food, and the body than clothing? . . . But you seek first the kingdom of God and his righteousness; and all of these things shall be abundantly added to you."

Humanity has never been able to understand how practical and real in experience are these sayings. Is it because man has never been able to learn the basic realities of human life? Some of these imperatives may sound to us impractical and harsh, but to Jesus they were practical and easy. Not even all of his disciples were able to live up to them. If men would only learn not to think of themselves but to think of others, no one would have to worry about tomorrow or bury his money. If the employer would work for the good of the employee, and the employee strive first for the interests of the employer, there would be no troublesome problems of labor, poverty or theft. If the producer and the consumer considered first the interests of each other, a large part of the wearisome burden of business would be eliminated; men would soon learn to trust one another.

Jesus illustrated his argument by pointing to the birds of the air and the lilies of the field as the highest examples for humanity. Through unheralded centuries the birds and other forms of what we term lower creation have developed their own peculiar social life. How often do we fail to realize that these creatures live a more peaceful life than do human beings! They seem to be content with their manner of living. They are close to nature because nature is their only God and house of refuge, and its laws their only governing powers. On the other hand, during his progress man has revolted against nature. He has defied its laws and tried to invent religions and gods to suit his fancy.

While passing over the hills near Galilee lake, Jesus saw the lilies growing wild, their blossoms watered with dew which had fallen during the cool night hours, their roots in the ground toiling day by day and waiting for the rain and sun from heaven. In Palestine lilies are not cultivated as they are in America. They flourish in their own natural habitat, unmolested by human cultivation.

Easterners have no knowledge of plant life. They have never studied biology. They do not recognize that these creations of nature are "living." They call these forms of life instinctive, because so little is known about them. But dumb and silent as they are, the wild flowers share in our creation and progress. The workmanship of the Heavenly Father is recognized and his love and care abundantly expressed.

The birds and flowers of today live under the same natural conditions and environments as their ancestors thousands of years ago. Progress seems unnecessary. Barns, treasures, and selfish gain for which a man will sell his soul seem not to concern them.

Man, however, has never been content with his natural life; he must advance, and over the path of his progress his own artificial world has been created. He lives under unnatural conditions, such as were not intended for his well-being. He eats foods which were not made for him to eat. He violates natural laws, and then makes his own laws and religions to protect the violations. He works and saves; he instructs his generation to climb still higher up the path. He digs gold from one part of the earth, and buries it in another part. If the birds and other lower forms of life watched all the evil things man does, they would think him an "instinctive" form. They would conclude that he has to cheat, kill, rob, and bury his money because he was made that way.

VII. Oriental Hospitality

"Who is among you who has a friend and he shall go to him at midnight, and say to him, my friend, lend me three loaves, for a friend journeying has come to me and I have nothing to set before him? And his friend from inside would answer and say to him, Do not bother me; the door is already locked and my children are with me in the bed, and I cannot get up and give you. I say unto you that if because of friendship he would not give him, yet because of the urgency he will rise and give him as much as he wants. I am telling you also, Ask and it shall be given to you; seek and you shall find; knock and it shall be opened to you. For everyone who asks, receives; and he who seeks, finds; and he who knocks it is opened to him. For who is among you, a father, if his son would ask him bread, why, would he hand him a stone? and if he ask him for a fish, why, would he hand him a snake instead of a fish? and if he ask him an egg, why, would he hand him a scorpion? So, if you who err know how to give good gifts to your children, then, how much more will your Father give the Holy Spirit from heaven to those who ask him?"

An unexpected traveler came at night to a certain house, and the master of the house found that he had no bread. He dressed hastily and went to his nearest neighbor, knocked at his door and asked him to loan him three loaves. "We have had more strangers than we expected today. Another guest has just arrived. We have not enough bread to serve him and to provide for his journey. Please get up and loan us three loaves."

Three loaves were needed because the guest had arrived at night and was to depart early in the morning. If he had arrived in the daytime and was to eat at the house, more would have been borrowed and put before him. A guest is embarrassed if it is not possible for him to leave many crumbs on the table after he has finished eating. If one leaves no crumbs on the table, he is supposed to have taken away the blessing of the house; he will never be welcomed again in that dwelling. The beggars are the only ones who leave no crumbs.

Customarily, three loaves are given a departing guest. This is just to carry him to the nearest town, one loaf for each meal. Travelers need leave no crumbs. A child is allowed two loaves a day; a woman three, one for each meal; a workingman six; a shepherd seven. To an honored guest the whole supply in the house is given. Nevertheless, a guest of reputation seldom eats more than half a loaf.

The borrowing of bread is an ancient Eastern custom. No one can bear to refuse loaning bread to his neighbor, for some day he himself may receive unexpected guests and no one will lend to him. Even the richest people of a community will borrow bread. It is loaned and returned with many compliments from borrower and lender. There are times when one lends ten loaves to his friend, and in return receives the same number, but only half the weight. In such cases shrewd women refuse to lend to certain houses whose credit has thus been lost.

In the East every family expects guests to

enter without notice, day or night. In countries where hotels and restaurants are unknown, and where hospitality necessarily dominates, people believe that it is a sin to sell bread. Strangers and travelers are welcome. Every man eats his share. "A house without guests is a house without blessing." "Today he is our guest; some day we may be his." "Cast your bread upon the waters and you will find it again," means "be generous to strangers."

Early in the morning, when the women prepare the dough, a few extra handfuls of flour are thrown in as God's share. "Let that be for the strangers." Before it is mixed, the sacred name is invoked. "O God, make this the share for the strangers and the needy. Bless it and increase it."

Housewives can generally identify the knock on the door. They can discriminate between the knocking of a traveler and of a beggar. A beggar knocks with his stick on the ground, and in response comes a woman or a girl, who brings him a piece of bread; the guest and traveler knock on the door with their sticks or with a stone. What Jesus said applies only to guests, travelers, merchants, and preachers. He never encouraged men to beg.

VIII. Rich Men

It was on the shores of Jordan, near the border of Judæa, not far from the place where a few years before John was baptizing and preaching the gospel of repentance. The multitudes had gathered from the near-by towns of Judæa. Pharisees and scribes had come from Jerusalem to hear the new prophet, whom the public proclaimed successor to the Baptist. The echoes of John's message were still heard. The voice of the man whom Herod beheaded was still whispering in the ears of the simple villagers, who believed that John was raised from the dead. "Who knows? This man must be the Baptist. He resembles him in every way," said some of those who had been baptized by John.

During this period of his ministry, Jesus passed

into a new phase. He no longer had patience with his treacherous enemies; he would not answer some of the questions men asked him. He was bitter in his denunciations, and more versed in quotations from the Holy Scriptures. The Galilean who had preached meekness was now turned into a militant prophet. He seemed to depart from his own early teachings. He could silence the eminent scribes and priests with a few questions and rebukes. He even challenged Moses as a lawgiver. Moses, he declared, had made certain concessions in the law, not because he wanted to, but because the public insisted that he do so.

It was after the closing of such heated arguments and debates that one of the men who was impressed with his words suddenly rushed to Jesus and addressed him: *Malpana tava!* "Oh, wonderful teacher." "I believe you are the greatest man I have ever heard. I enjoyed all that you had to discuss. I have never heard another man say these things. You must be a man of God." Jesus, a little withdrawn and tired after the long and weary hours of talk and hunger, looked at him for a while. He then said gently: "Why do you call me wonderful? There is no one wonderful but God. I am not as you think. I am not a great teacher. God is the only wonderful teacher. What I teach is not mine, but is given to me by one who sent me. He is the only teacher who knows all."

The word *tava* in this case means simply wonderful in skill. If the man had meant good or holy, he would have used the word *kadisha*. *Tava* is used only when describing the quality of work, such as wonderful carpenter, wonderful shepherd, wonderful ox. A shepherd may be a criminal, but still be called "good shepherd," not because of his good character, but because the sheep follow him and he knows how to feed them. On the other hand, Jesus refused to accept the honor of the name "wonderful teacher," because an Oriental whose teaching is from God always tries to hide his popularity. The less he says concerning his knowledge, the more the people think of him; the more he hides himself, the more popular he becomes. The Pharisees and scribes, however, sought to be honored and called "wonderful."

With a touch of humor, Jesus then told this man that if he wished to enter into eternal life, he must keep the Commandments. He knew he was a believer in the law for salvation. "I have kept them from my youth. What else do I need?" Jesus replied that if he wished to be *gmira*, perfect in obedience, he should go and sell everything, and give all to the poor. This sounded very unpleasant to the inquirer, who had accumulated considerable wealth and was now asked to part with it on such short notice.

After the meeting the crowd gradually began to disperse. Jesus turned to his disciples and in a low tone said to them: *Amarna lkhon dadla ye latira Dneaol Lmalcootha Dashmaya:* "It is difficult for the rich to enter the kingdom of heaven." *Dadlil lgamla lmeaal bakhrora damgata au atira dneaol lmalcooth dalaha:* "It is easier for a rope[1] to enter the eye of a needle than for a rich man to enter the kingdom of God."

Christians in the Western World are often bewildered when they are confronted by these verses. Why did Jesus bar rich men from entering the kingdom of God? Can men live without money? Churches and religious institutions are built and supported largely by contributions from rich men. Indeed, this saying did not refer to the rich men of all lands, but only to the brutal rich of the Orient.

In the East, almost invariably, a rich man ac-

---

[1] This word also means camel, but rope is more appropriate in this connection.

quires his wealth not so much by his profession or hard labor as by force and extortion. The rich man harvests where he has not sown; he gathers where he has not reaped; and by the virtue of his wealth he becomes an overlord, too superior to bear burdens like those borne by the common people of his town. According to Eastern tradition wealth is a blessing from God. Nevertheless, most Orientals would never wait to be blessed from above. They bless themselves by unjustly acquiring property belonging to the poor. The sooner they are blessed the better they like it. Abraham, Isaac, Jacob, and Job were blessed with abundant wealth. When God made a man rich, "let us keep him rich," say the Easterners. On the other hand, the poor man is cursed and kept in poverty, because to help a poor man to become rich is against the will of God.

As soon as an Easterner acquires money, servants, and lands, he is exempt from all local and government taxes. Furthermore, by accepted custom, he levies special taxes on the poor of his town whenever he pleases. When other rich men come to visit him, he seizes the sheep of the poorest people in his town to make a feast for his honored guests.

A poor man is allowed to beg only crumbs of

bread left at the tables of the rich. The rich men are also beggars. They are the only ones permitted to collect money when their revenues fall short, or when they intend to add a few more women to their harems. One can frequently see a stranger entering a town, accompanied by scores of armed servants riding on beautiful horses. He is a rich man from another town who has come to beg on his arrival. He is met and escorted to another rich man's house, and immediately the latter begins to collect sheep, oxen, and money from the local poor to be given to his visitor.

Jesus saw the greed of these rich men, the ways by which they built up their wealth, and the heavy yoke they forced the poor to carry. Solomon was the richest king in Israel. He was supposed to be blessed by God and in favor with God. David, his father, however, had destroyed nearly all of the small kingdoms in Palestine, killed their men and plundered their lands. When he died he left countless treasures of gold and silver. A small part was dedicated for use in the sacred temple, but God refused to accept his share of the wealth which David had so unjustly acquired. Later he consented to accept it from Solomon, who had not participated in shedding the innocent blood of women and children of Canaan. When Ahab ruled the northern kingdom about a hundred years later, he desired to bless himself in order to win the hearts of his people, but there was nothing left to possess through spoils. There were no more small kingdoms to conquer and so he killed his own subjects in order to inherit their properties.

The parable of Lazarus and the wicked man is based on the imagination of the Easterners, who protest and seek vengeance in their hearts against the evils of the rich. On this earth they can do nothing against a rich man, and have to be satisfied with the hope of justice in the hereafter. They picture the man who had plenty on this earth and who had unjustly confiscated their property, as facing starvation and punishment in the other world, where the poor would at last be blessed with abundance. But this prospect does not in the least trouble the rich man, who thinks he is on this earth to enjoy life. "Who knows what the other world is?" he sneeringly asks.

When I was a boy I often heard one of the modern and popular Eastern parables concerning the rich man. In this parable the wicked man was an Armenian broker and merchant, who had acquired a great fortune by loaning money at one hundred per cent. Through his prosperous business he had saved everything he could and spent little. The rich broker believed only in receiving from others. He never gave a cent away. He even suffered personal deprivation in order to save money. One day he entered the safety vault to see the piles of gold which he had accumulated. Suddenly the secret and intricate steel door locked behind him, imprisoning him helpless with his own treasure. Later he was found dead with a note in his hands: "All this gold I would have given for a glass of water and a piece of bread."

Government and public officials in Bible lands are always elected from the ranks of rich men. Corruption and injustice to the poor prevail as a result. The priests and rabbis are but instruments in the hands of these men. Where much money is, there sooner or later are also power and corruption. "Where there are corpses, there gather the eagles."

When the rich and the virtuous are placed on the scales, one always rises, the other falls. So, at last, instead of having contentment and glory, men become lovers of trade and money; they honor and revere the rich man and make a ruler of him, dishonoring the poor man. Think of what would happen, said Plato, if the pilots of ships were chosen according to their wealth, and a poor man was refused permission to steer, although he were a better pilot.

IX. "Let the Dead Bury the Dead"

In the Near East, when two strange men meet, the conversation generally begins with inquiries as to their places of abode: "Where do you come from? Where do you stay? Are you married?" An American lawyer would not ask half of the questions which are asked of a casual stranger there.

A man asked Jesus such questions while he was addressing the crowd. Jesus knew what was in the heart of this man; that what he wanted was to follow him because of his popularity. Jesus said to him, "The birds have nests, the foxes have holes, but the Son of Man has not even a place to put his head." Another said to him, "Master, I will follow you, but let me first bury my father." This means in Aramaic, "I have to take care of my father, who is an old man." Jesus replied, "Never mind your father. The town will take care of him. You have relatives and friends; they will feed him and when he dies they will bury him."

Plainly this man's father was not actually dead. If he had been, the son would not have been able to go out and listen to Jesus, and Jesus could not have spoken in the town on that day and insulted this man by telling him, "Let the dead bury your father." Nothing could provoke the indignation of an Easterner more than such a remark as, "Let the dead bury your father," if a man's father had really passed away.

According to burial custom, preparations are made as soon as the eyes are closed; sometimes patients have only lapsed into unconsciousness. The dead are buried as soon as the grave is ready. If a man happens to die in the morning, he is buried before noon; if he dies at noon, he is buried before the sun goes down. Often men and women are buried alive. At times they get out of the coffin when the procession is marching to the grave, while the priests are chanting and the mourners are following the coffin. The dead return to life with a sneeze! This accidental burying of men and women alive, and their revival with a sneeze, have been common matters among the Assyrians and other ancient people, who understand nothing about modern medical science. The Kurds break the backs of "dead" men for fear they may sneeze and come back to life. They believe that the evil spirits have taken possession of the dead body. The Assyrians give them another chance to live. I myself attended the funerals of two girls and one or two men, who got up from their coffins before they were put into the grave.

Jesus knew what this man meant. "Let me bury my father" signified in English: "My father is an old man, over seventy years of age. I have to support him until he dies." When a man reaches this age he is considered dead. He has finished his work and has no more interest in life. He can no longer earn and produce. He is a burden on his family. He entrusts everything to his oldest son, his first born, who is to continue his posterity. He has labored and toiled with the sweat of his brow, and raised his children. Now he expects them to take care of him. One often hears Easterners say, "My father is near the grave!" or, "My father is at the side of the grave." If literally translated it would mean: "My father is dead and is put in the coffin, and the coffin is waiting beside the grave to be lowered." But the real meaning is: "My father may die any day. My father is very old; I expect him to pass away any time."

Generally when a father is very old and not feeling well, his oldest son would not consider leaving his home for a long journey, because the deepest desire of an Eastern father is to have his son at his bedside when death approaches. Nothing is of more comfort to a dying parent than to look into the face of his first-born son, who is to carry on his name. When death approaches, the father while lying on his sick bed formally blesses his son and entrusts the family to him. It is, moreover, the father's desire that his son should close his eyes on his death-bed.

Jesus weighed all the responsibility that this man owed to his father, and he knew that a son's burying his father was a mere custom, another tradition of the elders which so-called pious Jews would not break.

The Aramaic word for "dead" is *mitta*, and the word for "town" is *matta*. There is a slight difference in pronunciation. On the other hand, in many of the mutilated manuscripts the small Aramaic character which determines the difference between the meaning of these two words, is destroyed, especially in cases of carelessness in writing and because of the glossy manuscript ink used. Furthermore, in the early centuries, the Aramaic language had no vowels. One would easily confuse the meaning of words which had a close similarity in form, especially at a time when there were no scholars or grammarians, and every man wrote and spelled as he pleased.

Consider, for example, the Aramaic word *tlita*. It means "little girl" and "sleeping." In such a case not even the Aramaic-speaking people would be able to determine what Jesus meant when he said to the daughter of Jairus, *Tlita koome*, whether he meant, "Little girl, arise," or, "O thou that sleepest, arise." The correct meaning of some words has thus to be determined only by the context of the sentences or through the manner of expression. So also what sounds like a harsh counsel rather expresses confidence in community responsibility, when Jesus said, "Let the town bury the dead," which has been unfortunately mistranslated "Let the dead bury the dead."

X. Days of Gloom

It was the month of April, the hot season in Judæa and the only unpleasant time of the year. The harvest had just begun and the fields were yellow. There were a few spots of green grass in the valleys where the water had not completely dried up. The roads from the north and east were crowded with caravans carrying new fruits and sheep to the Holy City, to be blessed in the temple.

The Feast of the Passover was nearing. The Jews everywhere were making preparations to celebrate once more the exodus of their forefathers from Egypt, and the lamb which was sacrificed on that epochal night for their salvation.

Jesus also decided to leave Galilee on his way to Jerusalem. He had determined to face his enemies and accusers. He had preached enough to the peasants of Galilee. Now he wanted to see if he could move the arrogant hearts of the priests of his Father. But there were no signs of encouragement; fortune did not favor him.

He was not quite decided what to do, and so he urged his disciples to go to the feast, declaring that he was not yet ready, for his time had not come. He would rather miss the sacred feast than face what looked like unavoidable embarrassment. He knew that his enemies were spreading a net for him in Jerusalem, but on further consideration he saw there was no alternative for him. He therefore finally resolved to attend the feast. This was to be his last journey to the Holy City. It was the city which had crowned kings and killed prophets, and which was to crown him on the cross. "O Jerusalem, Jerusalem, murderer of the faithful!"

During this journey Jesus kept referring to his death. "The Son of Man will be delivered into the hands of sinners. They will crucify him and on the third day he will rise again. You will see me for a while; you will seek me and you will not find me; then you will see me again." In the early part of his ministry he had spoken more about life and its purpose. Now he spoke about the end of the world and tried to impress upon the minds of his disciples that even the unconquerable Messiah must suffer death. It was all so confusing and discouraging to them. They had never really understood the meaning of "Messiah," partly because they did not understand his sayings and partly because of repeated disappointments to their literal hopes.

Jesus had hitherto not spoken in this strain. His discourse to the disciples and the public had been limited to the Kingdom of Heaven and the conditions of membership therein. His teachings were interpreted through picturesque parables, which pleased his listeners and augmented his audiences. The Master who a few months before had spoken comforting words and given strong assurances to the poor now became severe in his manner. The prophet who had gained notoriety for his gentle ways and meek spirit now assumed an austere tone. He had become like one of the old prophets, and not unlike John the Baptist in his denunciations of Pharisees and scribes.

His enemies had aroused his innermost soul and dared him to face them. The priests in Jerusalem had spied on him and reported his actions to Herod the tetrarch. Emissaries from Jerusalem had spread reports that he was not a law-abiding citizen. Some of his direct remarks against the priests and his new interpretations of the Scriptures had been laid before the high priests. Herod had sent men to see him, but Jesus had no fear of this king who had taken the life of John. He answered these men: "Go and tell that fox he need not trouble himself. I shall soon be out of his territory. I am in this world a few days more. I am on my way to Jerusalem."

Peter was more advanced in years than Jesus. More than the other disciples, he realized the seriousness of the situation and became uneasy. He began advising him, actually rebuking him a little: "Far be it from you, Master. Why are you saying these things about yourself? Don't you know you are wounding the hearts of your disciples? Some of the men who have followed you all these years may leave you at any time. You are the Christ, the Son of the Living God. Now you say you are to die. *Rabi la la,* 'Master, no, no.' Far be these things from you." Jesus' anger was now aroused even against the man he loved so much. Three years of continuous preaching had not changed Peter's mind or made him realize that the Messiah was to die in order to live and rule forever. For a while he kept silent, gazing into Peter's eyes, and hesitating. He did not wish to rebuke him, and for a while he could not control his indignation. Then suddenly his face turned crimson: "Get behind me, Satan, for you love things of man more than those of God."

These simple men, who once made a bare livelihood fishing in the lake near their homes, had left everything and followed him and were soon to be left as sheep without a shepherd. They had expected some day to sit on his right and left hand, to judge their enemies and be merciful to their friends, to become princes of their countries, to rise from fishermen and publicans to governors and chancellors. But the dreams of kingly rewards, which they had long expected from the man who had persuaded them by the sheer force of his touching words, who had not displayed desire for wealth or any ambitions for honor, were vanishing like a shadow at sunset.

Jesus' popularity was rapidly declining. The public had become tired of him. They wanted to see him do something besides preaching. Three years of suffering and of effort had passed, and nothing decisive had been accomplished. Some of the poor had come to him hoping to become rich, but they were now starving. His disciples themselves had become discouraged. Miracles, demonstrations, and enthusiasm had contributed little toward any lasting success. Men and women admired him, that was all, for they had no faith in him as a leader; he was not a business-like man; he seemed rather to be destructive than a builder. There were no symptoms of uprising among the ranks of his followers and admirers; no converts from the upper classes; no princely and priestly backing. Was nothing to be done to win the unresponsive hearts of his people except to die? To his disciples that resembled suicide, a way in which to escape the real problem. They were mystified about the future.

For a long time the priests and rabbis had made threats and had sought to lay hands on him, but they were afraid of the masses who still followed him. They had nothing specific against him, and to arrest an innocent religious man was a difficult problem. The public might make an issue of his cause and start an open revolt in the north. The warrior Galileans would riot at seeing their prophet arrested unjustly by the Jews.

Not very long before, he had raised Lazarus from the dead in a town a few miles from Jerusalem. This act made the priests and the Sanhedrin more restless and hostile toward him. They could not understand this man's acts; they could make nothing out of him. He certainly had some power, to perform these miracles, they said to one another. But how could this sacrilegious man come from God, when he defied God's own Commandments? He had been in the company of sinners; he would eat without washing his hands, and he prayed very little, if at all. The Sanhedrin met and decided they must somehow do away with Jesus or their whole career would come to an end. "We had better lose one man than lose our temple revenues," said Caiaphas, the high priest. "Don't you understand if we leave this man alone he will expose all our secrets? There will be many people who will go after him, and the country will be thrown into revolution?"

During his earlier ministry the High Council of Elders did not interfere with him. A poor man preaching to the poor! What harm could he do to them? He was not receiving any income from his speeches. Many of those who went merely to listen admired his teachings. But at that time Jesus had not attacked the religious leaders. His sermons had not aroused the poor against the rich. He had not created an organization to back him up. He was not trying to make reforms, demanding that certain changes in worship should be made. "Let him preach; he will soon get tired and so will the people."

Jesus now directed his main attacks against the leaders of the Jewish faith, the sacred priesthood of his own religion, and the traditions of its elders. The religious teachers, and those who acted as guides, he called blind. If blind leads blind, both will fall into the pit.

"Woe to you, scribes and Pharisees, hypocrites! for you defraud the property of widows with the pretense that you make long prayers; because of this you will receive a greater judgment.

"Woe to you, scribes and Pharisees, hypocrites! for you have shut off the kingdom of heaven against men; for you do not enter into it, and those who are entering you hinder.

"Woe to you, scribes and Pharisees, hypocrites! for ye traverse sea and land to make one proselyte; and when he becomes one, you make him the son of hell twice more than yourselves.

"Woe to you, blind guides, for you say, Whoever swears by the temple, it is nothing, but whoever swears by the gold which is in the temple, he is guilty.

"Oh, you blind fools, for which is the greater, the gold, or the temple that sanctifies the gold?

"And, whoever swears by the altar, it is nothing; but whoever swears by the offering that is on it, he is guilty.

"Oh, you fools and blind, for which is the greater, the offering or the altar that sanctifies the offering?

"Therefore he who swears by the altar, he swears by it and by everything that is on it.

"And whoever swears by the temple, swears by it and by him who dwells in it.

"And he who swears by heaven, swears by the throne of God, and by him who sits on it.

"Woe to you, scribes and Pharisees, hypocrites! for you take tithes on mint, dill and cummin, and you have overlooked the more important matters of the law, such as justice, mercy, and trustworthiness; which were necessary for you to have done, and by no means to have left undone.

"Oh, blind guides, who strain out gnats and swallow camels.

"Woe to you, scribes and Pharisees, hypocrites! you clean the outside of the cup and of the dish, but inside they are full of extortion and iniquity.

"Blind Pharisees, clean first the inside of the cup and of the dish so that their outside may be clean also.

"Woe to you, scribes and Pharisees, hypocrites! for you are like decorated tombs which look beautiful from the outside but inside are full of dead bones and all kinds of filth.

"Even so from the outside you appear to men to be righteous, but from within you are full of iniquity and hypocrisy.

"Woe to you, scribes and Pharisees, hypocrites! because you build the tombs of the prophets, and you decorate the graves of the righteous;

"And you say, If we had been in the days of our forefathers, we would not have been partakers with them in the blood of the prophets.

"Now you testify concerning yourselves, that you are the children of those who killed the prophets. You also fill up the measure of your fathers.

"Oh, you serpents, and seed of scorpions, how can you run away from the judgment of hell?"

No wonder they looked upon Jesus as another enemy of their race, an archenemy, who, in their minds, was attacking the roots of their religion and law, which seemed to be threatened with disaster. The Romans were trimming the branches. Their aim was to bring to an end the Jewish political and temporal power, exercised under the pretense of religious laws. This invasion of their religious rites, and the privileges which false traditions had bestowed on them, was more serious than the Roman subjugation. His teaching, healing of the sick, and cleansing of the lepers were attributed to the power of the devil. They doubted that these could come from God. They could not understand how this ungodly man could do these things in the name of the Living God, and yet show himself disloyal to the doctrines and traditions of their sacred faith. These clever Jewish diplomats had fooled governors and emperors, yet now they seemed to be defeated by a Galilean peasant.

At times Jesus was advised and warned by converts, lawyers, and friends who wished him to recant and change his attitude towards their religious worship and the historic priesthood. "It has taken us centuries to build up this system. We have suffered persecutions and slavery in order to enjoy our religious freedom and to keep the traditions of our fathers. We have drunk the blood and eaten the flesh of our fathers in building this temple, and you wish to destroy it and rebuild it in three days." To this charge Jesus replied: "Except you eat the body of the Son of

Man and drink his blood, you have no life in you."

The old covenant had failed to save the Jewish nation and to bring fulfillment of the promises made to the forefathers. "I am the new covenant. You must suffer for me. You must eat my body and drink my blood in order to achieve your complete independence and your religious freedom." "Eat my body and drink my blood" in the Aramaic idiom signifies "endure suffering and hard work." Moses had given them manna from heaven and water from the rock. David and Solomon had enriched their wealth as a nation. But these benefits could not help them to escape captivity and disaster during the centuries. This people needed different leaven and new bread, both of which were offered by Jesus, not only to them but also to the Gentiles who preyed upon the Jews for lack of spiritual and moral nourishment.

XI. At the Gate

It was his last entry into the city which he loved so much but now sorrowed to see. What a spectacular entry into the City of David! Before Jesus arrived at the Mount of Olives, a little group of friends and admirers, who had come up to Jerusalem for the Feast, had gone out a few miles to greet him. Other small parties, chiefly women and children, had left Jerusalem a little earlier to greet relatives and friends coming to the feast. Instead, they met the train of Nazarenes. A young man with a black beard and soiled old mantle was riding on an ass, surrounded by a group of poorly dressed followers and a few friends. Some of the men and women who had accompanied him from Bethany began singing "Hushana, Hushana, Hushana, the Son of David! The Mighty One, the Mighty One, the Mighty One, Son of David!"

The disciples were a little embarrassed and afraid to sing. Some of them were ashamed and fearful. They saw their Master was not entering the city as a conqueror, and they were aware that the noise and singing would cause trouble. This was the first public demonstration held on his behalf. The singers were not aware of the open hostilities between Jesus and the Sanhedrin, which was in session on the top of the hill they were climbing. These men wanted to cheer Jesus and show that they were with him. But his disciples realized that Pharisees and priests would not tolerate such an entry into the Holy City on an occasion like this. Thousands of men and women were now in the town. A rash remark could incite revolution. Other Galileans who had tried to capture the city had been defeated and put to death.

As the group of disciples and admirers began descending towards the city, it was augmented by more men and women who had come from Galilee for the Passover, and who wanted to make a triumphal occasion of the entry. There were others who mocked the spectacle. They laughed, made insulting remarks, and threw stones at Jesus and his disciples. Some would not even look at them. Jesus, riding on a donkey, advanced slowly into the city, painfully watching the crowds near the temple, occasionally looking at the housetops where crowds had gathered.

Jerusalem was gay. The Jews seemed to have forgotten their troubles. Jesus remembered prophets who had entered the Holy City, some of them only to be stoned. He could not restrain his emotions for these ambassadors of God who had met with this sinister fate. Disaster was soon to fall on what some of his credulous followers still thought was a triumphal entry. These staunch admirers fancied Jesus was to ascend the throne of David, to occupy the chair vacant for many years. But in the eyes of more respectable law-abiding, blue-blooded Jews, Jesus and his disciples were nothing more than a group of ignorant countrymen and beggars, who had come to the Passover to fill their stomachs rather than to worship. They had seen them come every year.

The entry into Jerusalem was different from what the disciples, especially Judas, had expected. Instead of a group of priests dressed in crimson clothes, with Jewish dignitaries and great officials singing psalms of triumph, "Arise, O God, and let thine enemies be scattered," they were greeted by a horde of common people, chiefly northern Galileans, who were called Gentiles by the Jews of Judæa. Most of them had known Jesus for many years. Some were men and women whom he had healed. Others were servants and slaves, surrounded by a fringe of Jerusalem boys who would not miss the fun. It was the shrill cries of these boys, which provoked the wrath of the priests and Pharisees, when the procession crossed the Valley of Kedron and was nearing the temple grounds. "Master, stop them. Don't you understand what these men sing? It is a sin. These are holy words only to be sung before the Messiah. What is all this?" These were the only greetings offered by the Jewish officials.

Jesus descended to the city by the way of Gethsemane and went straight to the temple. In the week of the Passover the streets were jammed with humanity; merchants of all kinds began annoying Jesus and his disciples. A group of thirteen men should be prospective buyers. They had not as yet bought anything. Other Jews were buying sacrifices and changing their money into temple coins—the only money acceptable to the priests, because coins bearing the image of a mortal were an abomination to the Jews. They also transacted other business which had to do with temple worship.

Jesus, accompanied by his disciples, went to the Gentile courts in the temple, where he could find a little space in which to speak. There, too, he was approached by scores of small peddlers carrying their trays of merchandise on their heads. They began closing in around him, and occasionally interrupted him in his talk, while Pharisees and priests frantically argued with him, trying to trick him into some damaging statement. Some of these men who gathered around him had seen him entering the city accompanied by the procession. They had followed him to the temple ground simply out of curiosity, while others openly insulted him. The once peaceful gathering had turned into a mob.

Jesus was filled with indignation and dashed the trays off the heads of the peddlers. In a little while the group was thrown into confusion and tumult. The dense crowd began to disperse. The merchants who owned the doves had no time to recover them. Trays of coins lay scattered on the ground and beggars scrambled to pick them up. The temple guards and established merchants who had rented booths were pleased because they hated these peddlers, who took business away from them and who conducted their business so dishonestly. Jesus did not interfere with the regular temple business. But the priests were angry at him. "What business has he to interfere with temple work? Where did he get his authority?" said some of them.

Everything appeared gloomy and disappointing to his disciples. Nevertheless, some of them took things fatalistically. The man they had followed had simply failed. He had done his best. But what can a lone individual do to a rockhearted people, whom God himself had not been able to master? For three years Jesus had worked miracles, healed the sick, raised the dead, done wonders before their eyes, but the people had not believed him. In the final analysis he had failed to hold his ground. His attacks on the priestly craft had only increased his enemies. Indeed, there was no sign of a weakened priesthood. The thousands who swarmed into Jerusalem had brought more sacrifices and gifts to the temple. There was more religious devotion than ever. The priests were highly honored and their blessings were sought by thousands. The Nazarene was shut off with his disciples in a small dirty inn. No one cared to visit him. Jerusalem was too crowded. He had to go to Bethany in order to find a place for the night. Yet he had been proclaimed the future ruler of his race! Forsooth, a King without a throne, a man without a country!

The Prince on that day was not the popular attraction of a year before. He had lost all his popularity. Three years of preaching and promises, only to be fulfilled after death, no action, no sign of political change, caused even some of his followers to desert the cause. Many of his friends lost faith in him. The nation was passing him by. That was nothing new. They had not really believed the prophets who had preceded him. There was nothing strange in the course of events which were taking place in the current prophetic history. Jerusalem had slaughtered other prophets. The Holy City would do away with him, too. Some of the disciples were buried in thought, murmuring to themselves, shaking their heads and once in a while shrugging their shoulders, wishing they had not come to the Passover.

Why had he jeopardized their lives for the sake of his own gains? Judas was brooding over his own hard fortune. He had left his own business, friends and opportunities, and followed a man whose own folk and townsmen had cast out. The other disciples were insignificant fishermen, most of whom had followed him only for the sake of their daily bread. They had lost nothing; they could return at any time to their occupations and easily borrow a few fishing-hooks. Judas was the greatest loser. In his eyes the wanderer had been a unique opportunity, offering a shrewd adherent possibilities of acquiring wealth and fame, friends and honors. This man who could heal the sick, even raise the dead, presented unlimited chances to make money. Men would be willing to give half of their possessions to be healed. But to Judas, Jesus had proved himself a mere idealist, not practical or shrewd enough to acquire fortune.

However, even now it was not too late for Judas to save something from the wreck of his hopes. He was a clever business man. He was in the movement for business and his mind always operated in a business-like way. He had lost opportunities and time, true; but he could revenge himself on this stupidity and he would even sacrifice his own son for that. Besides there would be some money reward. He might also secure immunity, even pious praise, from the heads of his religion by surrendering his Master into their hands.

During this whole week friends had begged

him to quit before it was too late, and to have the false prophet arrested and punished for his acts. Judas could then easily induce the Jews to believe that he was but a weak-minded enthusiast and had been seduced by a man of supernatural powers; that he was one of the thousands whom he had misled. He could also tell them that he had remained with the group only to bring them to just such an end.

Jesus and his disciples spent most of this week coming to Jerusalem and going to Bethany for the night. The city was crowded and they could not find lodging, so their friends at Bethany had extended an invitation to them.

While they were guests of Simon, the leper, a woman who had vainly sought to reach Jesus ran into the house, and poured a box of precious *nardin*, perfume, on the head of Jesus while he sat at the table, and washed and wiped his feet and dried them with her hair. Simon was displeased. It was an insult to him that a harlot had entered into his house and embarrassed him before his guests. What business had a woman to enter men's divans while guests were dining? But he was still more shocked by the attitude of Jesus. Why did he not rebuke her when she came near him? Why had he allowed her to put that oil, which she had bought with impure money, on his head? However, Simon held his peace. He would not embarrass his honorable guest.

Jesus was pleased by the generous act of this woman. He had come from a long journey, and was tired from sleeping in the caves and on the road. His clothes had not been washed. The oil refreshed his head. This was the only gift which the woman could offer for her sins. But the strange ceremony caused indignation on the part of the fishermen, who had used nothing but plain water to wash their faces and heads. There was a tense feeling among all the guests. They were surprised at the sight of the precious perfume. They began whispering. Why not pour a little on their heads? Why not have it sold and given to the poor? "Waste, all waste," exclaimed some of them. Here was a good excuse, an occasion for Judas to protest against the lavishness of his Master, who had told them they should not save silver or gold, nor carry two shirts, but ignore the luxuries of life. Surely he was departing from his own simple teachings. The disciples for a while murmured to themselves; then they began to talk to one another about the oil. *Mishkha tava*, "Precious nardin," they kept repeating the words. Then Judas boldly began to rebuke the woman. "Why trouble this woman, for she has done no harm but good things for me?" said Jesus.

Apparently Judas was more disappointed and angry because the oil had not been turned over to him to be sold. Money in the common fund, and himself the treasurer, was his idea. His heart became so filled with hatred toward his Master that he was no longer held by the sacred bonds of Eastern discipleship. He could wait no longer. He had lost all faith, and the few remarks of rebuke which Jesus made were sufficient to ignite his burning heart. After all, what good would a few drops of oil have done him? He had expected rewards far greater than the gifts of kings. He had hoped that some day his uttermost desires would be fulfilled. The man he had followed for three years was to become ruler of Judæa and finally a ruler of the world. Then Judas would have power to punish his enemies, to confiscate properties and lands, to have many servants. In this crisis, the three years of wandering with the Galilean dreamer seemed to him as an early-morning dream. His aspirations during all this time faded. His Master was far from what he had expected him to be. He was naught but another dreamer and revolutionist, without enough courage to die on a battlefield with honor. Judas lamented the three precious years which he had lost and in which he had gained nothing. The cold nights in the winter and the hot Palestinian summers, the thirst and hunger which he had stood—that memory brought no consolation to his heart but rather indignation over what he regarded as the greatest disappointment that had befallen him. The sequel was, however, to end in the desperate tragedy of suicide.

XII. Washing the Feet

When Jesus was at Bethany, his friends urged him not to go to Jerusalem. They knew he would be arrested. Many of them had heard Pharisees and priests threatening to lay hands on him. They begged him not to attend the Passover that year. "Rabbi, you had better not go this year. Let us return to Galilee," said Peter brokenheartedly, the tears streaming down his cheeks. Not even his mother, who had come down to see him, or Mary and Martha, who loved him so much, could turn him from his determined course. His disciples perceived that the mind of their Master was settled and that he was soon to leave them.

While they were in Galilee the priests in Jerusalem had done everything to capture him. But in Galilee things were different; for there the priests had little influence. Besides, the people of Galilee were not on good terms with those of Judæa. Racial antipathy strongly prevailed. The Galileans despised the southern Jews who had yielded to Roman and Herodian terms just for the sake of retaining temple revenues. Moreover, most of these northern regions were more or less annexed to the Roman province of Syria. Jerusalem was the capital. The temple, which had become the most sacred and important institution in the life of the nation, was identified with the great Sanhedrin. The ruling Senate was also in the Holy City. The Romans were diplomats. They had to please Jewish ecclesiastical authorities in order to be able to rule the rebellious Jews of the south. What of it, if the Sanhedrin petitioned the Roman governor to arrest and kill a Jew of their race? The Romans would gladly do it.

As the time drew nearer, the disciples began reasoning things out for themselves, thinking of their own future. "Suppose they arrest him and kill him, and as a result, the public rises up against the priests! Granted that chance might overthrow them. Who will take command? Who will be the successor?" Jesus had never chosen a successor. He had promised that he would always be with them. He had spoken about his death, but he gave the impression that his death would be a victory; that only by his death could he triumph over his enemies. They hoped that he who for three years had been doing wonders, might at last work one great final miracle and strike the priests to their knees before him. Furthermore, they were told by some that the priests would not dare to arrest their Master, fearing an uprising and a bloody revolution.

Then again they felt that while dying he might show supernatural signs which would win people's hearts to him. They thought perhaps he would die just to arouse public sentiment to fight for his cause. There was nothing strange about that. Men who did very little and were hardly known during their lives had often exerted much greater influence over their followers after death. John, who a few years before was a hated man, was now accepted as a prophet. The Jews lamented his death. But John was put to death by the order of an alien king, a grandson of an Idumæan usurper. The public could never tolerate the killing of a prophet by the religious leaders of their own race. Especially a lovable man like Jesus! His disciples were to take his place and to carry on his work.

Who, then, was to be at the head of the movement? Who had enough courage to lead the people? Matthew understood the government. He had spent most of his life as a publican and politician. As a diplomat perhaps he could persuade the people; possibly he might organize, purchase supplies for armies, and make treaties and intrigues. So he doubtless thought. Peter declared, "To me he has intrusted his sheep. I must feed the sheep and lambs." John suggested, "I am his best friend. He has promised me that I shall sit on his right hand." Jesus heard most of this conversation, but kept all these things in his heart and waited for the supper to come, at which time he would reveal to them the secret of his ministry.

It was Thursday, Passover Day. They left Bethany and ascended the Mount of Olives. Jesus then instructed two of his disciples to go to the city and prepare for the Passover. "You will find a man carrying a pitcher. Follow him. Wherever he enters, you enter, and tell the honorable master of the house to prepare one of the chamber rooms for the Passover."[1] Jesus had lodged in this public place, *balakhana* or coffee house, on many other occasions when he was in Jerusalem. The place was largely patronized by Galileans and foreigners. He knew the proprietor and the manservant who carried water and served the guests.

Water is invariably carried by a woman, except in the case of a public house for men. The guests at a *balakhana* are men; a female servant cannot be employed in such a place. Most of those who had brought their wives with them had secured lodging in the houses of friends and relatives. Perhaps this was the only house in Jerusalem which had a place for guests who had no women with them. In the East, who would dare to invite thirteen single men to his house, even if all of them were saints?

It was late afternoon. Most of the streets were deserted. A few Gentile merchants and Roman soldiers were the only people in the streets. Jesus and his disciples entered Jerusalem quietly. The city was silent; the flickering lamps of Jerusalem were the only signs to be seen. Everybody was at home, ready to eat the Passover with haste,

---

[1] In Aramaic "good" is *tava*, and in this case it means honorable.

to repeat the custom which their forefathers had performed two thousand years before.

When the time came and supper was ready, Jesus and his disciples, according to custom, sat on the floor in a circle in one of the small chambers. Because the bread is considered sacred, Easterners believe that it is sinful to put it on the table, or to sit on a chair while eating. The devil will find a place to sit underneath. Knives and forks must not touch the sacred bread; it must be broken by hands only. Tables were unknown to them, and are still unknown in some Eastern countries. The little group of friends sat down, their feet folded under, their hats on their heads, and their shoes removed. It is considered unlawful to remove hats while eating, or to sit at a feast with shoes on. The servants began to bring the Passover dish, lamb, wine, and unleavened bread. This was the food which every Jew was to eat on that evening, and Jesus was to eat it for the last time with his disciples. An earthen cup, a little jar filled with wine, two or three large dishes, according to the size of the group, were put on the floor over a table cloth, called *pathora*.

Two dishes and two wooden spoons are considered sufficient for ten guests. Each guest eats with the spoon when his turn comes, and passes it to the one who sits next to him. They all drink from the same cup. This is not because of the custom, but because of the scarcity of dishes, earthen cups, and spoons. Easterners neither believe in nor are afraid of germs.

The cup was put in the center near everyone in the circle. The jar was placed near Jesus. He had to pour the wine and drink first. Before they were ready to eat, Jesus began washing the feet of his disciples. He took an apron from the servant and girded himself in a manner which disturbed Peter. "Master, not me. I would not have you do it." But Jesus began to explain that the greatest man among them was to be the lowliest, that he who was their teacher was now to be their servant. He had told them not to call anyone rabbi; not to seek political power; for the kingdom of their Master was not of this earth. There were no temporal positions for them to seek. This was the answer to the disagreements concerning leadership which had troubled them at Bethany. Jesus was ready to wash the feet even of Judas.

*

XIII. The Betrayal

It was a day of joy to every Jew, and all Jerusalem was prepared for the Passover. Some of Jesus' disciples forgot for a while the foreboding conversation, and were happy. Others were sad as they sat eating and watching their Lord, who talked about his death, partly to himself, but once in a while to them. "Verily, verily I say unto you that one of you will deliver me up." They were shocked and filled with fear. They took their hands from the dish and began gazing into one another's faces. "Am I he, Master?" asked Judas. Jesus replied, "The one who puts his hand in my dish." That was Judas. He was sitting close to Jesus, but he was eating from other dishes, too, occasionally eating from the dish before Jesus. Judas' color changed. He had

THE BETRAYAL

acted strangely the whole week, but he wondered how his Lord had found out his secret plans.

In the East servants are always very careful in arranging dishes. The best dish, with the more delectable food, is always put before the leader and those sitting near him. At this end of the table, food is more abundant and richer. But guests do not hesitate to stretch out their arms to other men's dishes. Dishes are exchanged, bread is passed around, meat is wrapped in thin loaves of bread, put into pockets, and carried home. The worst breach of etiquette is when a guest passes his sop to his friend. According to common superstition, a sop half-eaten and then passed means a breach of friendship between the two men.

In the course of the supper Jesus took bread and broke it, saying, *Sow akhul hana pagre,* "Take and eat; this is my body." He glanced at the lamb which they were to eat. The lamb is regarded by all Jews as symbolical of the salvation of their race. In the eyes of Jesus this lamb was nothing but the meat of a dumb animal slaughtered against his will. "This is nothing; do not think any more about this lamb. This rite is doomed. No more lambs, no more sacrifices. God is tired of the blood of animals sacrificed every day. Forget about Egypt. The lamb of Egypt has not freed you from the bondage of sin. You have never been a free people. Right now you are under the Roman yoke. You are slaves to your sins. This lamb has served your fathers temporarily, but hereafter I am the Lamb. I am the Lamb of God; the Lamb which humanity has chosen to offer to my Father. This is my body, an everlasting sacrifice. Why should innocent animals die for the sake of sinful men? Hereafter when you do this, do it in my memory."

While they were eating he took the jar and poured red wine into a cup, omitting the exchange of formal greetings with his disciples. The wine which makes every man's heart merry was made for Jesus a cup of sorrow. The wine resembled blood which he was to shed on the cross. It was not like the blood the Hebrews put on the entrances of their homes before they left Egypt, to distinguish the Hebrew homes from the Egyptians. His blood was to be a new covenant, not only for the Jews, but for all mankind. *Sow eshtaw minney culkhon. Hanaw dem dad-yatekey khdata daglap sageye miteshed lshokana dagtahey:* "Take and drink from it; this is my blood of the new covenant which is shed for the sake of many for the remission of sins." Jesus had often drunk this cup in memory of his people's salvation. He would have his disciples drink it henceforth in his memory. The emphasis in the Aramaic is on *kolma*, "whenever," which means "When you do it next," or as often as you do it in the subsequent years.

Jesus knew that on that evening the Pharisees and high priests were also to drink the same cup. But to them it was a cup of victory. At last they had conquered their enemy, who was seeking to destroy their long-established business. They had nothing to say about Egypt. As far as they were concerned this religious festival had lost much of its significance. What they were worried about now was the Prophet of Galilee, the pretender to the chair which they were occupying.

The Aramaic phrase, "This is my body and this is my blood" carries the meaning directly to the lamb slain centuries before in Egypt. Even though Jesus was pointing his finger at the elements which stood on the table, the words led the imagination of his disciples back to the origin of this ancient custom, the flesh and blood of a lamb their fathers had eaten hastily while they were leaving their land of exile.

The sun had sunk behind the hills. The brilliant Palestine skies had become dark, and twilight hung on the horizon. The Feast of the Passover had ended. A place of rest would soon have to be found. Jesus and his disciples, except Judas, retired to Gethsemane, a garden on the northeast side of the Valley of Kedron, looking towards the temple. Most of the people in the city were asleep, except occasional travelers, shepherds who were watching their flocks, strangers who had not been able to find a place of abode, and the high priests who were awake, holding a council.

Jesus left his disciples at the garden near the valley, and climbed the slope to the top of the ridge looking towards Jericho, far away from both enemies and disciples. A wonderful place to pray, and a good place to escape if necessary. He kept praying. The bitterest time in his life had approached. His hour had come. He must either be delivered into the hands of men or plunge over the summit and disappear; but this latter would be cowardly, especially for a Galilean. His disciples slept. They were weary and could not watch and pray.

That silent hour of prayer and agony, and that evening in Gethsemane, the long hours of loneliness! Jesus was meeting his second temptation. It was an hour when he was to decide his future.

His earthly end had come. One of his own disciples had turned against him. The rest were disappointed and peacefully sleeping. The world was passing before his eyes, with the devil who had tempted him in the desert standing before him once more. The temptation was doubly strong this time. Now Jesus was not hungry for bread nor had he the desire to be ruler of any kingdom.

Men have fasted more than forty days and lived. Kingdoms have been lost, honors declined, crowns renounced, but life is more dear than the whole world. Rich men will lavish their millions if their life can be prolonged for another hour, but to Jesus death was life. Failure was triumph. Physical and material matters had no hold on him. He was only concerned about the soul which death cannot destroy. Death, which men called a calamity, was to be for him a real victory. Hitherto, he had appeared before the eyes of his disciples and they knew him as a living man, but soon he was to be worshiped as a God. Jesus was just beginning to live and to write a new religion in the hearts of men. In the past he had lived in obscurity in the hills of Judæa and around the Sea of Galilee, but now he was to live in all the world and in the hearts of men.

During those silent hours of prayer, Jesus was to determine whether he would live for himself or live for the world, whether the voice which had whispered into his ears at the River Jordan was the voice of God or just an echo coming from an empty cliff. The prophets had predicted a suffering Messiah. The Scriptures must be fulfilled. If God was with him, what difference would it make whether he was alive or dead? Moses had died about twelve centuries before, but now he was living securely in Jewish hearts. When he was alive he was hated, his Commandments broken. Now he was loved and his law strictly observed. Jesus himself was to die because, in the eyes of the Jews, he had not respected the law and observed the Sabbath as they thought he should.

This was the biggest opportunity for his adversary, the devil. There was another adversary, perhaps superior to the devil—sinister death, which took his toll of the human race. This fearful enemy of mankind was now hanging over him and waiting for the nails to pierce his feet and hands. For a while Jesus thought that perhaps he could escape by descending from Gethsemane to Jericho and crossing the Jordan into the desert. Who would find him? Then he began consulting himself. His human body was making every protest and resistance. The body was weak but the spirit strong. "Why should I die for this kind of people? What would my friends think of me? My mother would be disgraced, and the shock of such a death might kill her. The people will always think I was wrong, and therefore met with such a death. Why should I be killed by the people of my own faith? Why should I be branded a traitor, a blasphemer? They will never understand my side."

While praying, groaning and thinking, he was disturbed by a small noise caused by the dry leaves on the ridge, or by travelers coming from the north. He hurried back to his disciples. "Arise, let us go, for he that is going to deliver me is coming." They awoke, but they saw no one. He went back again to pray.

While praying, Jesus turned his face toward Jerusalem every once in a while, and any sign of light or sound of a voice brought more fear to him. He instructed his disciples to sleep while he continued to pray. Kneeling on the white stones of Gethsemane, Jesus was again submerged in thought. He saw the symbol of his cross standing before his eyes, and he himself hanging on it. He had seen other Galileans shamefully executed.

Two Jews who had been arrested were to be crucified after the Passover. On the other side stood the Son of mankind and humanity to be saved. The devil who had tempted him in the desert was also there, but this time he made no effort to tempt him. He stood over him as a victor who had conquered his enemy; with his hands folded on his breast and with a pretended sign of sympathy for the one who had not listened to him. "If you had taken my word, you would never have reached this end. You would have been the greatest figure in this Feast. Instead of being greeted by that insulting procession of boys and beggars when you entered the city, you would have been received with open arms by the priests."

But Jesus kept praying silently, with tears in his eyes. *Ave, in mishkha nibran casa hana bram la akh dinna, savena ela akh datt:* "My Father, if it is possible, remove this cup from me; but let not my will but thine be done." He was to drink a cup which the priests of his Father had filled with poison. He had been proclaimed a king, only to wear a crown of thorns. For a while he was lost in thought about his disciples and his mother whom he was to leave behind.

THE BETRAYAL

Life was dear to him because he was dear to those who knew him.

There was more to be done, but he could do it afterward. He was not afraid of death which destroyed only the body. The fearful *Sheol*, the land of shades, cannot hold him. It cannot separate him from the Living God. He could have escaped with his disciples to places where his enemies could never have pursued him, but for him everything was over. His hour was upon him. He had come to Jerusalem only to die. There was no better place than Jerusalem for this kind of death.

It was nearly nine o'clock in the evening. In the East people retire early: they go to sleep when the sun sets and get up when it rises. This was a late hour to be outside, according to the custom of the quiet city. But they were not to wait much longer. In a little while the temple guards and servants of the high priest began descending from the temple grounds, holding lanterns in their hands, to cross over the Valley of Kedron and into the Garden of Gethsemane. Jesus saw the lamps flickering. In a few minutes the officers, accompanied by Judas, were in the Garden, looking for Jesus.

"Whom do ye seek?" he said to them. "Jesus of Nazareth." He replied, "I am he."

They rushed against him as if to arrest a criminal. But Jesus, in gentle words, told them that he was the man they wanted and begged them to let the others go. The guards were astonished at the humility of the man. They had expected that the Galilean would resist to the last, but they soon found that their swords and knives would not be needed. Jesus did not offer any resistance. In a few minutes his hands were tied behind him and he was brought into the palace of the high priest.

Immediately some of the servants went and awakened members of the Sanhedrin who were not at the council, and asked them to assemble at once in the house of the high priest. Some of these elderly men did not know why they were called at such a late hour. They did not know who Jesus was, had never heard of him. "Which Jesus?" they asked the servants. "Rabbi, the man from Galilee. The man who has been creating disturbances among the worshipers." While entering the council chamber they saw Jesus, surrounded by guards, waiting in the outer room to be called in. As soon as they were assembled Jesus was brought before them. The high priest cried aloud to make them hear him. "This is the man, Jesus of Nazareth, a Galilean, who for years has disturbed the peace of the nation; the man who has been trying to starve us and our families." Jesus stood silently in the middle of the circle-like divan, while the members of the Sanhedrin lay on silken cushions, their faces gazing upward into the face of the prisoner.

To Jesus this was a unique occasion. For a while he forgot what was going on and why he was standing there. The solemnity of the hour overshadowed everything else. While they were talking he kept staring at them, as if he were not concerned in what they were doing. Some of them thought he was crazy; others thought he was merely terrified. It was the first time in his life that he had seen close at hand the high priests and the rulers of his race. That same formidable high priest whom he had glimpsed from afar, moving about and chanting Scriptures in the Holy of Holies, was now on a soft cushion before him, sitting in judgment.

For a while he studied them. He watched every move of the high priest and those who sat near him, but before his eyes this holy group of pious men was not better than a herd of unreasoning beasts. They were high in ecclesiastical officialdom, but low in character. They were supposed to be the custodians of the sacred books and of the law, but in reality they were leaders in imposture and ignorant of the Scriptures and truth. Most of them, especially the leaders, had fattened on the sacrificial meat. They secretly ate the best part of what was supposed to come as a special offering to the golden altar. They drank the holy wine and ate the bread which were put in the Holy of Holies. They never worried about anything except when they divided fat temple profits, for then they often cheated one another. There were thousands of less fortunate ecclesiastics who shared these temple privileges, and who were making an easy living under the guise of "priests of God."

After brief court formalities, all manner of accusations and false witnesses were brought against Jesus, but he answered no questions. Why should he answer? When the high priest asked him why he did not reply to the charges against him, Jesus replied, "If I told you, you would not believe me, nor would you let me go." Then the high priest cut him short. They must compel him to say something in order to convict him. He put him under the sacred oath and made him swear

THE BETRAYAL 117

in the name of the Living God. "Tell us, art thou Christ, the Son of the Living God?"

The time had come for Jesus to speak. He could no longer keep silent. But he would not answer yes or no. "Thou sayest". The Aramaic *Att amaratt*, means "*You* say that," "I do not clearly understand what *you* mean by the 'Son of God.'" Jesus knew they had only understood him literally. Pagan religions had a strong influence in Palestine at this time. Roman and Greek gods had wives, concubines, and children. Jesus being a Galilean and virtually a Gentile in the eyes of the Jews, what he taught about God was suspected by them. Although the Jews spoke of God as Father and men as his children, they were intolerant towards all pagan conceptions of gods, who were conceived and born like human beings.

There was a pause. Jesus must answer now or deny the title, and yet he must answer them carefully. "But I say unto you that from now on you shall see *Lawrey d' nasha*, the Son of Man, sitting on the right hand of power, and coming in the clouds of heaven." The priests had now heard with their own ears and there was no necessity for further questioning. His claim to sit with God was sufficient to convict him.

Jesus did not answer directly. If he had, the answer would have been *"Aen"* which means "Yes," or *"La,"* which means "No." *Att Amaratt* is not a definite answer. It rather puts the question in doubt. Jesus was not trying to hide that he was the Son of God. He knew why the high priest put him under oath when he asked that question. According to Jewish law it is unlawful for a man to make himself equal to God. The blasphemer is punished by death. The old high priest had not understood Jesus' meaning of Son of God and Fatherhood of God. Jesus was not willing to convict himself through the theological ignorance of his accusers. That would have been worse than suicide.

The Jews had long before lost their political independence, therefore they had no power to put any man to death. That was something which only the Roman governors could do. Thus, in accordance with the law, they brought other witnesses to testify that Jesus had said he was a king and that he told the people not to pay head taxes to Rome; that he had incited rebellion in Galilee and throughout Judæa. These were serious charges because they were political. Accusations that he had said he was the Son of God or that in the other world he may sit on the right hand of God, were immaterial to the Roman procurator, who himself could say that he was a son of the Emperor. In the eyes of millions of Roman subjects, Tiberius was a greater god than Jahveh, whose people and land the Romans had conquered.

Jesus was led out of the palace to an adjoining room so that the priests and members of the Sanhedrin should not touch him. He was a condemned man, and anyone who touched him, even by accident, would be defiled during the week of the Passover. The servants passed the early morning hours mocking him, bandaging his eyes, striking him, and bidding him prophesy.

It was during this time, while Jesus was leaving the high priest's palace to go to a servant's chamber, that he saw Peter and heard the denial. One of the women doorkeepers had seen Peter with Jesus and had recognized him. She told him that surely he was one of the Galilean's followers. Peter denied, swearing and cursing, that he had ever met or known the man. When she saw him more clearly, she cried out that he was one of them. One of the men verified this by Peter's speech: he spoke Galilean Aramaic. The Jews in the South spoke Chaldean Aramaic. The dialects differed to the extent that the differences were noticeable.

Early on Friday morning the procession began to leave the house of the high priest, wending its way towards the governor's palace. Some members of the Sanhedrin, with a group of scribes and prominent Pharisees, marched ahead, accompanied by Caiaphas, the high priest, and followed by the palace attendants. Jesus came next, surrounded by temple servants assisted by some of the temple guards.

The procession marched towards the palace of Herod, now occupied by the Roman governor. The narrow streets were jammed; men and women stood on the house tops. Masses of humanity began to pour out of the tiny houses of Jerusalem. Some of them stared at the procession, wondering what had happened in the silent hours of the night. They had known nothing. The Passover had occupied all their thoughts. Women with their hands covered with dough went out to see what was going on in the street. The feast and temple worship were forgotten before the magnitude of the colorful procession of Jewish dignitaries, unique in its character. All political parties had joined together. Enmity between the two rival houses of Annas and Caiaphas was also forgotten. It seemed as if some glad news, the tidings of freedom, had arrived from Rome.

The procession forced its way through the solid masses which were standing before the palace. It was an impressive spectacle. What could be more thrilling in the eyes of the onlookers than a simple shepherd, who through some misunderstanding had been proclaimed a political king, who had aroused the indignation of the people and now was ready to go to the cross!

Some of the men shouted: "Who is that man? Is he the one who a few days ago entered at the head of the Galilean party?" "Yes, he is that man, the one who calls himself Christ the King," replied some of those walking behind the solemn procession.

XIV. Before Pilate

The palace door opened and the high priests and their party entered. Then Jesus was brought before the governor. The ruler of this world was to judge the Prince of Heaven. Jesus seemed more cheerful as he entered the palace of a foreign governor, an oppressor of his people. He felt more at home here in the house of this pagan than in the "Holy Palace" in which the treacherous priests lived. There he was in the hands of a band of fanatical murderers. Jesus was weary. He had spent the night without sleep and had suffered insults and punishments.

The high priests and their party waited in one of the reception-rooms, while Jesus was taken before the governor in one of the executive chambers. The Jews could not enter there, because it was Holy Week. They might by accident touch unclean men and behold forbidden images.

Jesus had never seen Pilate before, and Pilate had never heard of Jesus until awakened early that morning from his sleep by the servants and the messengers of the high priest, and informed of what had taken place during the night at the palace of the high priest. The cold Roman procurator was moved to sympathy for the lean and haggard figure which stood before him. But this feeling soon changed into a burst of anger against the members of the Sanhedrin.

"What have I to do with a case like this? Am I a priest?" the governor muttered, partly to himself and partly to the servants and guards who stood before him in military state. He had expected to see a man who possessed all the characteristics of a strong revolutionist, whose fierce face would reveal his crimes, a statesman and diplomat in the rough. This was the sort of a man who could become the leader of bandits. Instead he saw a far different type from what his servants had portrayed to him in words. He saw the finest face he had ever beheld. There was nothing in the eyes to reveal crime; nothing in the face but love for humanity. His simple clothes, torn by the hands of temple guards; his sore feet and weakened body, did not reveal anything that resembled a criminal.

The procurator gave Jesus a new name—"The Man." "Is this the man you have captured? Is this man a leader? You call this man dangerous? You call him a king?" Pilate was deeply disappointed and his wrath was aroused. For a while he thought the high priest had done this purposely, had invented something to incite the Jews against Roman rule. Not a long time before, the Jewish priests had petitioned Rome to have Pilate removed from Jerusalem. He had taken temple money and used it for building a conduit, by which he brought water to Jerusalem. Many other false charges had been brought against him. The priests had been at odds with him during all his governorship in Jerusalem. They were a troublesome lot.

For some time tranquillity had reigned in Palestine, even though Messianic aspirations had lured many credulous men into banditry. There had been no rebellions of serious nature. Pilate had received no report from the civil and military authorities stationed in Galilee concerning the activities of the Man against whom the high priests were pressing charges of treason. The governor hid his feelings behind his dominating personality and executive demeanor. Then, according to the formalities of the law, he began asking Jesus questions: "How long have you been in Jerusalem? What do you sell? What damage have you done to the temple? Where did you come from?" What else could Pilate ask him? He knew nothing of the coming of Christ, nor did he care what this Man's belief was in God, or to what Jewish sect he belonged.

For a while Pilate kept moving about the room, trying to find an answer to give the high priest and the Jewish delegation which was waiting for him. Finally he entered the reception-room. The Jews rose and saluted him according to their custom, bowing their heads down to the ground. A moment of silence followed and a few minutes' exchange of greetings. Then the procurator addressed them in a low tone hardly concealing his anger. He was not able to hide his feeling for the Man, whose life was in his hands and in whom he had found no fault. "I have examined this man. I find he has done naught to warrant punishment by death. Politically, there is nothing I can do. Take him and judge him according to your own law."

The high priest answered: "If this man had not been guilty, we would never have brought him here. We are the soil under your feet; we are your servants, as you know. We would not accuse this man if we did not know that he is worthy of death. This man has stirred the whole nation from Jerusalem even to Galilee, preaching against the government, inciting revolution, proclaiming himself a king, and telling people not to pay taxes. What more evidence do you need? We have no authority to put him to death." The ecclesiastics disguised their real reason with this political camouflage, which was the only way they could gain their evil end.

Pilate for the first time now found some ground on which to question Jesus. As soon as he came back to him, his first question was, "Art thou the King of the Jews?" For a while Jesus was silent. The Easterner believes that the less he says when accused of a crime, the better chance he has for freedom. A man might convict himself by a word uttered unknowingly or unintentionally. "By their words they shall judge them." The eagerness of the governor for an answer, and his sincerity in trying to save him, made Jesus reply, *Min nowshakh emart hadey o'khraney emar lakh aley:* "Do you say that of yourself or have others told you concerning me? My kingdom is not of this world." "You can see what kind of king I am. Ask yourself, do I look like a king? If I were a king, my servants would have fought for me so that I should not be delivered into the hands of the Jews."

Pilate pressed on, "Then you are a kind of king?" "*You* say that I am king. I am not. I was born and came into this world, only to suffer and testify to the truth. I am standing before you in this manner in order that the truth might be known to the world. If I had not unveiled the mysteries of religion, if I had not attacked the corrupt practices of the priests, I would never have been brought before you."

"What are these truths?" asked the governor, abruptly—which means, "What are the principles which you support and for which the priests are accusing you?" The governor did not wait for an answer. He knew that the whole affair was a frame-up. The battle between Jesus and his countrymen was caused by theological questions. Pilate was both ignorant and contemptuous of Jewish dogmatic theology and traditions. Let them settle their differences among themselves.

The governor found there was no crime committed, which warranted death on the cross. Therefore, partly to avoid responsibility and partly because he was persuaded by his wife and some of the palace servants, not to have anything to do with the blood of this man whom the palace officials believed to be innocent, Pilate sent Jesus to Herod, who at that time was in Jerusalem, and under whose jurisdiction Jesus was. Jesus did not answer Herod's questions. That would have been useless, since Herod would do anything to please the priests and Pharisees. He had had John, son of a priest, beheaded for defending the Mosaic law. Why should he let a Galilean usurper and a heretic escape the penalty? Here was a chance for him to absolve himself from the innocent blood which he had shed, simply by imposing the supreme penalty on another innocent man.

Pilate then ordered the soldiers to scourge him, thinking that the cold Jewish hearts would be softened. But the Jews continuously cried out, "Crucify, crucify him. Let his blood be upon us and our children. We have no other king but Cæsar."

XV. On the Cross

It was on a Friday afternoon. The excitement of the Passover had subsided. The city was quiet. Some of the men were leaving, others preparing to leave, but the majority stayed to watch the greatest spectacle of the whole week. The free drama which the priests were to present would surpass even that at the amphitheatre. Three men were soon to be nailed alive to crosses.

The forced trial was concluded in great haste, that the condemned men might be crucified and buried before the Sabbath. The procession left the governor's palace, Jesus bearing his cross on his shoulders, surrounded by Roman soldiers, temple guards, and a long line of Jewish dignitaries, rabbis, and high priests, who followed him to Golgotha. The hills on the outskirts of the city were crowded with men who had come early in order to find places near the crosses. The distance from the Holy City to Golgotha is not very long, but the road is rough with stones, and hard to travel because it ascends. This hill, in shape, resembling a man's head, was chosen because of its advantageous position. The crosses could be seen from the house tops and streets. Women who could not walk in the midst of a dense crowd could look on from the city and watch the three condemned men die.

The cross proved too heavy for a man who had been tortured for three days at the hands of temple guards and soldiers. Jesus was weak. While climbing the steep hill, whenever the long end of his cross touched the rocks in the road, he stumbled until he was unable to carry it. The punishment he received during this hour was more than what he had suffered at the hands of soldiers during his hours of trial. Hitherto only soldiers were allowed to scourge him, but now everyone who wished, took a share.

On arrival at the place of crucifixion, the soldiers hastily planted the crosses, undressed the victims, and began their work. There was nothing more to be done. No further questions were to be asked. Sabbath was approaching and the work had to be done quickly. The executioners waited for a few minutes for hammers and nails to be handed them. First the two bandits were fastened to their crosses. Their execution aroused little curiosity. These men were dying because they had broken the laws of the Empire. In the eyes of the Jews they were unimportant. The soldiers had little difficulty in crucifying them. The rabble stood far away.

But when Jesus was ready, the soldiers had difficulty in keeping away hundreds of priests, scribes, and Pharisees, who had to spit on him and say *Demakh breshakh*, "Your blood be upon your head." They had Jesus already tortured before the soldiers could raise him up on the cross. Even saintly Jews, who would have avoided hurting an ant, spat on his face and struck his head. Jesus was condemned for blasphemy, he was a heretic, an enemy of their God. And this severe treatment was considered an act of piety by these fanatical Jews.

Jesus was soon nailed on the cross, his feet and hands fastened so that he could not escape. The blood began pouring on the green grass and on the white stones, which resembled small altars. There was nothing for him to do but to wait for the end. Life was gradually ebbing; the strong body which had endured years of suffering began to weaken. Those penetrating brown eyes which had discovered the sting of death, even though tired from sleepless nights and blinded with blood from the wounds on his face, were still open only to see the ghastly end. Jesus beheld every move of those around him. At one time he moved his head and looked on both sides. He gazed at the malefactors crucified to right and left; he wondered why these men were dying, then he looked at the temple and the Holy City in the distance. A few days before he had seen thousands of lambs, sheep, and oxen slaughtered for the sins of his fellow men. Now he himself was sacrificed.

Near his cross stood some of the dignitaries, rabbis, and ecclesiastical leaders who had argued with him and accused him. They had come from Jerusalem to see their enemy dying, to see if the healer of others could now show miraculous signs. Excited provincial Jews, in concealed sorrow, were watching one die whom they had hoped would ascend the throne of Israel. It was a great day for Alexandrian and Roman Jews who were attending the Passover. The Roman soldiers and the temple guards stood patiently witnessing the last breath.

Those Jews who arrived late came straight

forward, close to the cross, and cried: "O destroyer of the temple, and builder thereof in three days, release thyself if thou art the Son of God, and come down from the cross. You saved others, why cannot you save yourself?"

One of the thieves crucified with him also reviled him. This man shared in the excitement and for a while forgot that he likewise was on a cross. Indeed, he and his companion had escaped the attentions of the crowd because all the interest was centered on the middle cross.

Tumultuous crowds of Jews of every degree, who had gathered around the cross, talked freely about Jesus. No one dared to speak a good word for him. Some admittedly showed a little sympathy; others concealed their feelings and looked on coldly, while yet others cursed him aloud. "We told you he was a deceiver, that he was not the Christ. There is the man. What a Christ! What a Saviour has come to save us! He was only a pretender, a blasphemer. He had not even the little courage of a bandit, to die with honor. His evils have brought him to this end. God has punished him."

A few of his disciples, hidden in the crowd, were stunned by the sudden calamity which had befallen their leader. Some of them forgot that they had anything to do with him. The man who for three years had aspired to long-cherished Messianic hopes, and proclaimed himself the mighty deliverer, was crucified with bandits and had met with the death of a malefactor. Truly they were disgraced. Why should they share in this guilt? The sooner they could clear themselves, the better. They even doubted that he was the Christ or had the least resemblance to the man they had hailed three years before.

Jesus heard everything that was said. His body was tortured with punishment and weakened by the loss of blood, but his mind was clear. He perceived every thought in the minds of those before him. The doubts of his disciples inflicted deeper wounds in his heart than the nails and spear in his body. He scrutinized the faces of those who were discussing him, but he said nothing. He had spent three years preaching, but he had not succeeded in softening their hearts. What could a few minutes on the cross accomplish? Those precious moments in his life were kept for prayer and thoughts of his mother, who stood with bowed head amid the jeering crowd.

There was Jesus, the King of Israel, the Ruler of the World, hanging on the cross, his name written in three languages—Hebrew, Greek and

Latin: "This is Jesus the King of the Jews." Hebrew was the holy language of the Jews read and understood only by them. Greek, the language of commerce, was used by foreign merchants and a few cultured Jews in business and social transactions. Latin, the language of diplomacy, was used by the Roman imperialists and militarists in government affairs. Jesus was a victim of priests, business men and politicians. He was soon to be proclaimed King of the World in all these three languages. The priests, the wealthy and the rulers were to be sanctified by his cross. The dreams of prophets were to be fulfilled. The visions of emperors who aspired to a world empire were to vanish. A new King was to be inaugurated. Soul had triumphed over body; the spiritual over the material. The powers of the earth were soon to bow down to the Prince of Heaven. The cross was lifted up to stand forever.

The silence which Jesus had maintained during his trial and on the cross amazed those who knew him. He who only a few days before had defeated the most eminent lawyers in the historic city could no longer speak in protest or defense. He could not rebuke those who accused him of falsehood. He did not curse those who insulted him. He would not perform a miracle and thus prove to the people that he was innocent. His agony and suffering in the last hours overshadowed everything which passed as a panorama before his eyes. His sorrow at those false priests, who during the whole week had purified themselves and offered thousands of burnt offerings, only to participate in an innocent murder, made him forget himself. In the eyes of the Jewish spectators, who waited patiently all evening, watching him dying, he was paying the supreme penalty for his blasphemous teachings. But in his own mind he was raised on the cross, like the serpent which Moses raised in the wilderness. Through his death he was to reveal the secrets of the sinister *Sheol*, Hades, and open a new way to immortality.

Jesus had no answers to the accusations and insults, but he was soon to answer briefly and finally, and only to his God. *Eli, Eli, lmana shabachthani* in Aramaic means, "My God, My God, for this I was kept." "This was my destiny. I was born and brought up for this hour, to be crucified for the truth. Let them say whatever they please. Let them think of this hour in any way they wish. Let them interpret it in their own way. As for me, it is all over. I understand why

ON THE CROSS

I am here. I have done thy will and I am here dying in accordance with that will."

The Aramaic word, *shabachthani*, means to keep, to preserve. The last words which were uttered through the lips of a dying man were not strange; they were words of consolation which any Easterner might utter when he is suffering and is resigned to die unjustly. This is the same answer which he made to Pilate when he was asked, "Why don't you speak? I have power to release you or crucify you." Jesus replied that Pilate had no power except the power which his Father had given him, and that he was born for this purpose.

How could Jesus have questioned God? How could God have forsaken him? What would his own disciples, who stood near by, have thought if he had implied that God had left him? Such an utterance would have meant a victory for his enemies and an end to those who still had some faith in him. The Galileans who were standing near the cross understood him because he spoke in their language. But the soldiers and others who stood near him could not understand the provincial Aramaic and they thought he was calling to Elijah. The word *Eli*, God, and the word *Elia*, Elijah, sound very similar in Aramaic, especially when they come from the cold lips of a wounded man over whose head hangs death.

Jesus did not quote the Psalms.[1] If he had quoted the Scriptures, the words on the cross would have been uttered in Hebrew and not in Aramaic. In that case Matthew would have added, "to fulfill the prophecy."

It is incredible that Jesus should have doubted the wisdom and power of God at this supreme moment, after having proclaimed throughout his career that he was in the closest harmony with the divine will. This was not a confession that God had forsaken him, as the popular versions imply. It was an acknowledgment that God had at last fulfilled his purpose through the death of his Son. It was not a cry of fatalism which expresses despair that all is over and there is no help for it. It was rather an announcement of faith in God, in the secure confidence that his death would bring the ultimate victory of truth, since truth is great and it must prevail.

The death of Jesus was to transcend physical limitations and make vivid God's revelation of redemption and his eternal purpose through a new beginning, to extend his spiritual influence

---

[1] The everyday common speech of Hebrew and Aramaic speaking peoples, even in operations of buying and selling, in its form suggests the language of the Scriptures.

over all mankind. His death was indeed the key to open the doors into liberty for all peoples. A glass of water placed in the Sahara contains all the qualities of water, but it is isolated. Ships cannot sail over this small amount of water nor can the fish live and swim in it. The moment this water evaporates it becomes an integral part of all water in the air and the ocean. Such is it with man who is alive physically but is isolated spiritually until he comes in contact with other spirits. This is how Jesus thought of his death. It was an ending of his physical part, but a larger beginning of his spiritual personality, which was to break through all barriers of isolation and win for him a following of loyal souls from every country and century for evermore. This is what brought him to Jerusalem. His death was the fulfillment of his destiny, and his last word had the note of triumph in God his Father, the Consoler of his soul.

XVI. The Resurrection

Darkness had fallen on the proud hills of the lofty city. Jerusalem was silent. The babel of merchants in narrow streets had subsided. The feast was over. The exciting and dramatic hours of the crucifixion had passed. Most of the Jews who had come from a distance had left. The others were preparing to leave soon. Priests and elders were back at their homes, resting, and discussing with their wives and friends the interesting drama they had seen and enjoyed. They had had no rest since Thursday night. During the trial the high priests had no time even to eat and to purify themselves. Now they were leaning on soft, silken cushions in their palaces. They had discharged their sacred duty in defending the faith. They had won what they thought a unique battle in the history of Israel. Hitherto there had been many political uprisings and intrigues, to overthrow their kings and to change their form of government. No one had ever dared to revolt or try to reform the Mosaic religion and law, without first winning a political victory over the state. Jeroboam and Ahab had accomplished this feat as rulers of Israel. But none of the great prophets had dared to make such an attempt. Indeed, the actions and utterances of the Nazarene were the first open attacks ever made against the holy priesthood, without political backing. Who could protest against the evils of the priesthood and escape punishment? A few remarks spoken carelessly against the priests had cost even rulers their crowns.

The shepherd was smitten and his sheep scattered. The Nazarene revolter was conquered, put to death, and his band of followers disbanded. The Jewish ecclesiastics were congratulating the false witnesses and temple guards for their hard labors and faithfulness. Everyone seemed pleased. What other proof could the public want from the high priest? The mysterious man whom he had condemned and sent to the cross was to them only a pretender. If he had been Christ he would have come down from the cross. The self-proclaimed unconquerable Messiah, who was to subjugate the nations of the earth, had died without any protest or resistance.

Satisfaction at the death of the enemy of their religion did not last very long. Uneasiness appeared in the faces of some of the shrewd dignitaries. The more they thought about the death of Jesus the more they were troubled at heart. They had done their duty, in ending the career of the man who had come from the North. But they had sent to the cross a man of their own faith, who had not offered the slightest resistance against his captors; who had not uttered one word of protest during his trial, except when struck on his cheek by one of the servants who had no judicial authority; a man who had willingly carried his cross. Indeed, Jesus, as they saw him dying, was far different from the dangerous man of whom they had heard so much. Uncertainty and fear now possessed them as some other facts arrested their attention. The man whom they saw going to the cross, as a sheep to the slaughter, resembled the picture of the suffering servant predicted by the prophet Isaiah. They were afraid he might rise, as he promised his disciples he would.

On top of the hill of Golgotha, a short distance from the city, stood three ugly crosses, stained with blood. Two men had died to satisfy Roman authorities, one to please religious officialdom. All three were Jews and members of the Jewish faith. The first two had conspired against political authorities, the third was accused of blasphemy. The "Lion of Judah," imprisoned in the grave, was soon to rise in victory.

Within the walls of the city a few of the disciples and friends still remained hiding in khans. The rest had made a hurried journey northward towards Galilee in order to escape arrest. Some of them had already borrowed nets and boats and had begun their fishing. Although bewildered, they still had faith in their Master. They had lost time in following him. He had given his life to make the local Jewish faith transcend its old boundaries and become the faith of the world. A high priest would give his life in defense of his religion for the sake of his official position and honor. Jesus had left nothing, only a destitute mother whom he had entrusted to the care of one of his beloved disciples. Even his few garments were divided among the soldiers.

The most faithful ones among his followers could not believe that their Master had left them. He whom they had seen nailed to the cross had raised the dead and opened the eyes of the blind. How could he die? Stunned as they were by the disaster which had befallen their leader, most of them could hardly remember what had happened on Friday afternoon. They could scarcely believe that their Lord had died. The occurrences dealing with his arrest, trial and crucifixion had taken place in such rapid succession, during such excitement, that they could not recall just what had taken place. In khans and other places, people conversed concerning the death of the Nazarene, which was broadcast all over the country. Some strongly condemned him, others praised his daring courage and gracious works, and still others knew not what to say.

Meanwhile his disciples were passing through confusing experiences. His life had come to an end, but they could not believe that it was all over. He said that his death was the only way to victory, that he would rise again, that he would return to them. Some could not believe that he who raised the dead would sleep in the grave. Others of them felt assured that he was not actually dead. They had seen him on other occasions escaping from his enemies. Why not again? Some of his disciples had disappeared since Thursday night, but they returned to Jerusalem on Saturday.

Waiting in disguise at the *Balakhana*, the inn, their powerful, penetrating Oriental imagination pictured Jesus standing before them. In other words, they themselves were raised. Their Lord was really dead and their hopes of the kingdom of earth had vanished. With their dreams of material aspiration shattered, they began to reason spiritually. The more they thought of Jesus the better they now understood his teachings. When he was with them they took his sayings literally. Now they saw more clearly. The kingdom of heaven which he had proclaimed was the everlasting kingdom. Earthly kingdoms were to pass away, and all peoples were soon to bow down to the Prince of Heaven. The temporal life was to be incorporated with the life everlasting. Their Master had shown them the way. He had gone to prepare them a place in this everlasting kingdom. He had given humanity new hope, and death new meaning.

Other religious movements either triumphed or went down during the lifetime of their founders. When the founders died, their followers were separated from them forever. But the religion of Jesus was the religion of the Living God. He had promised his followers to be with them forever. Death could not separate him from those who loved him. The unconquerable *Sheol*, which the Jews thought was not within the jurisdiction even of their God, was to be conquered, and its closed doors opened. This sinister *Sheol* held its grip on the people. When a Jew died, leaving no male issue, he went to this land of silence and sleep, where he was cut off from his God.

The salvation of the individual depended on the continuity of the state. The dead lived in and through their posterity. There was no resurrection. When the Messiah should come, those who were living would be organized into an everlasting kingdom. Such was the Hebrew conception of death, which made it hard for the disciples to believe that their Lord would surely rise.

It was late on Saturday evening, the beginning of Sunday. In the East the day is reckoned from sunset to sunset. The quiet holy Saturday had passed. The streets of Jerusalem were again filled with men. Caravans were preparing to depart for their destinations.

Out of seclusion and mourning three women walked quietly. Their heads were covered in black; their eyes watched every man who passed them. They were Mary Magdalene, Salome, and

Mary the mother of James. They were on their way to the grave to pay their last respects to their Beloved One. It was the beginning of the third day. The spirit of their Lord was to return once more to its body, but only for a few minutes. The belief is still held that the spirit of the dead returns on the third day to say farewell to the body. Relatives and friends of a dead man wait at the grave on the third day, to be once more in the company of their kin returning to visit them. This ceremony is customarily attended only by women, who encircle the grave, crying and talking to the dead one, calling him by name.

The women disciples would not miss this occasion. They wanted once more to cry out at the grave. But this time their Lord was to hear them, and though they could not see him, he could see them. On arrival they were disappointed; the grave was open. An angel had removed the large stone and sat upon it. At first they thought that the body had been stolen. The Jews had appealed to the governor for rigid vigilance over the grave, fearing that his disciples might attempt to steal the body. The few faithful followers who had remained in Jerusalem also thought that the fanatical Jews, whose hatred was kindling, might secretly remove the body to an unknown place, so his disciples would not find him or try to make a shrine out of his sepulcher.

Disappointed and bewildered by the disappearance of the body of their Lord, the women stood timidly gazing in one another's faces, shaking their heads and at times looking mournfully at the empty grave. They had come to say their last farewell to their Beloved One, but Jesus was not there. "Where is he?" they began crying and questioning one another. The Jews could not have taken him away, for they would not touch a dead body. Who else would steal him? Then the angels who stood in vigilance over the empty sepulcher told them that their Lord had risen and would meet them in Galilee, and that they should go back and tell the rest of the disciples.

This is the vital testimony which the disciples of the living Jesus have borne in every successive generation up to our own day. And please God, they will continue to do so to the end of time. The fact of the Risen One is the glorious assurance and the permanent hope of the Church. This is the conquering truth that makes life worth while, here and hereafter.

www.ingramcontent.com/pod-product-compliance
Lightning Source LLC
Chambersburg PA
CBHW031711230426
43668CB00006B/181